Blessings in Disguise

Early Sorrows and Lasting Miracles
in the town of Las Vegas, New Mexico

To Danelle Enjoy Blessing 11/28/11

J. P. Baca

J P Baca Thank you

ISBN: 061547067X
ISBN-13: 9780615470672
Library of Congress Control Number: 2011926407

"…The true story of my life and hard times and the blessings that came to me when I let go of the past and turned my eyes to the light that was always there."

Dedication

My book is dedicated to my Father and Mother.

William A. Baca served honorably in the U. S. Navy

My loving Mother, Margaret Martha Griego Baca

The Black Hell Hole Deepens

As a young boy I hated the home and family I was born into. I felt so alone, lost and condemned to failure.

Why shouldn't I feel that way? I had been told all my young life that I was not worth a damn. My Father's famous words were always the same — "You'll never be worth a damn and you'll never accomplish anything in life." *"No vas owf cumplir nada en tu vida".*

He said the same things to my brother Fred, and most likely to all the other children in the family. These words were rammed into my head so many times, that I began to believe his every word. This made me hate myself and my life even more. When a parent or mentor does this, it really kills a child's spirit, clips the wings we were meant to fly with.

In life, the actions of one—affect many!

As a young boy I'd often run away from home. Well, not really *run* away but just *walk* away without any direction, usually ending up on a bench at the plaza park where I hung my head and cried, making sure no one saw me. I simply wanted to get away from home. I wanted to kill the yelling. I wanted to disown the horrible feeling that I was no good, useless, betrayed, abandoned, and as I walked, I talked — "I hate you, I hate you. I hate my life and I hate who I am. Why wasn't I born to another family, another home, another world, another time?"

Even at that time though, and at that young age, I used to ask myself, "If I ever get out of this mess I'm in, what type of work could I do to earn money? And who would ever hire me?"

I was smart enough to know — confused though I was — that to have a real job, you needed to have training, experience, skill. This worried me. I didn't know *anything* about anything. And then I'd wonder — "If I were lucky enough to get married, how on earth would I support a wife and family?" These unanswerable questions gnawed away at me.

At that age I wasn't aware that my mind was only telling me what it was already programmed to believe and act upon. We do that to ourselves, you know. In life, the biggest enemy is us, not someone outside of us. We are conditioned to feed whatever negative image we have of ourselves and that is just as destructive as what someone might say to us. I'd swallowed my Father's negativeness, hook line and sinker, and like the proverbial fish, I was caught on an invisible line of doubt, insecurity and dependence on whatever he said.

Sometimes, however, I felt sorry for my father. I didn't know what type of upbringing he came from. Was his spirit also broken at an early age? I didn't know for sure but I figured it must have been. What's that saying? *As we are treated, so we treat others.*

What I knew about my Father when I was young, I knew very well indeed. He was a man who was full of anger. To relieve the fury within, the hatred of himself, he drank heavily. Even then I could see that he was resentful of anyone who'd gotten further along, who'd gotten ahead, as we used to say.

Of course he felt inadequate as a husband, father and provider, and naturally he felt he had to make everyone else feel the same way so that he could prove that he was the dominant one. These things seem almost rudimentary – to an adult. But though I felt them, I couldn't see them clearly; I also couldn't see any kind of solution for him, or for the family. To add to the confusion I felt, there were times when my father was also a loving and caring man.

When we were babies, and later on too, he would play with us. I can still hear his friendly laugh as he played with me. But by the time I was ten, my father began to shut down; at that age he couldn't, wouldn't, or didn't know how, to relate to me. Then, when I was a teenager, the severity of his punishments and my beatings increased. I guess he felt that as you got older, you could take more pain.

That's not to say that beating us was all he did to the family. When he was upset, my father started screaming, cursing. He had a sharp stare that cut you like a knife. You know that feeling in the pit of your stomach when you feel dangerously threatened? I felt that knife in my gut whenever he began screaming at us. And the more he yelled, the deeper the point went into my stomach.

There was a time when I wasn't permitted to walk to or from school because I'd gotten into some trouble at school. My probation officer, Manuel Valdez kept a close eye on me. My brother Fred used to drive me to school in the morning, home for lunch and then home after school in his 1955 Ford. I think I was in the eighth grade at the time. One day, while coming home for lunch, Fred and I noticed our dad pulling weeds in the front yard. When we saw his face, we knew how angry he was — angry and drunk, or maybe just hungover. His face always got red as a ripe tomato when he was in any of these conditions.

So this is what I remember from that time —

Fred parks his car.
We enter the house.
Sit down to eat.
Suddenly, kitchen back door flies open.
Dad storms in.
Plants a hard blow to my face.
Anger swells up in me.
I stand up, go at my father.
Father hits me, gets me in a choke hold from behind.
I push backward; we both slam against the kitchen door.
Fred yells — "Joseph, behave."
Fight breaks up.
I go sit in Fred's car.

After a while, Fred drove me back to school with no lunch in my stomach and an angry spirit full of hatred. The following day I saw Mr. Valdez and he asked right away, "What's that red ring around your neck?"

"My father and I got into a fight," I told him.

"But what's that ring around your neck?"

"I had my jacket on during the struggle and he got me in a choke hold from behind. My jacket zipper was cutting into my neck, and it left this mark."

Mr. Valdez told me to watch myself.

But, in reality, what I needed to do was watch my father and keep my distance.

For years I wanted to know why I was the victim of my father's rage.

Why the rage in the first place?

In the kitchen incident, later my father said I had hit my little brother Ereasmo, taken him by the heels and slammed him against a wall. This made my dad crazy.

But the whole thing was a lie against me and that was what hurt the most. I was blamed for something I hadn't done. Why?

Most of the time the bumps and bruises didn't bother me so much because, in time, they healed. What really hurt was the pain it caused inside. It takes a lifetime to heal that, as is evident by my writing this now after so many years.

And, today, it still feels like moments ago.

Walking around town I often found myself praying quietly. Not the pounding of the chest, making the sign of the cross ten thousand times a day type of praying, but the uttering of a simple, soft prayer like: "Help me God...and thank you for taking care of me."

I started going to church all by myself. One time I was sleeping over at my grandfather's house and Sunday morning, I rose early to go to church. I got up very slowly and quietly, so I wouldn't wake my grandfather. I quickly got dressed, washed my face, brushed my teeth, then flung my jacket over my skinny body, and walked out the door.

Man, why is it so dark? I wondered. It had never been this dark before when I got up at 6: a. m. to attend church. I hurried up the dark alley to Hot Springs Boulevard, turned left and walked swiftly to the corner of National Avenue on the Plaza. I stood on that corner looking west towards Our Lady of Sorrows Church.

There wasn't a single vehicle parked in front of the church, and I wondered if the services were cancelled for some reason.

After waiting for a while, I walked back to grandfather's home. The morning seemed really strange, dark and windy. When I got home, my grandfather was waiting for me. He explained to me that I'd misread the clock. I'd thought it was 6: a. m. but it was actually 3: a. m. when I went out the door. This was often how it was when I was growing up – the feeling of being in the wrong place at the wrong time.

I have always been an inquisitive person. As a kid, needless to say, this got me into lots of trouble with people but mainly with adults. I questioned anything I didn't understand, but particularly the hateful actions of those around me. Grown-ups didn't like this kind of questioning, especially my father. I also questioned God, religion, the teachings of the church, just about anything. With my dad there were no questions, only answers. *His* answers.

I didn't believe religious teachings because a man in a robe at the head of the church said it was so. I was never very trusting of people, in general, and even as a kid I could see that things were ordered in a certain way but not necessarily with the individual in mind. Society was in charge and lone individuals were like lone wolves — mistrusted by the majority.

I remember one Christmas holiday when I went to church with a few of my older sisters. After the church services, people were lining up to go and kneel and kiss the baby Jesus. The line was long and it was moving slowly. Finally, after a very long wait, I found myself with my sisters kneeling before the icon of the baby Jesus. Just like everyone before us, my sisters said a prayer, made the sign of the cross, leaned forward and bestowed their kiss. "*Andale* Joseph, kiss the baby Jesus," my sisters said impatiently.

No quiero, I don't want to.

Yes, you have to.

"*Por Que?* Look at all the kisses, all the lipstick on him, there's no place clean to kiss him," I complained.

So it went, back and forth. They all got mad at me and we went home and then these sisters told my other sisters, who were now getting ready to go to church and kiss the statue of baby Jesus, that I had refused to kiss the holy infant.

In the end, I was sent back to church with the second bunch of sisters and they were going to make sure I did the right thing. Well, they too found out just how stubborn I could be.

What did I finally do?

Well, if you think I kneeled and kissed him, you're wrong. I didn't. Too much lipstick and too many kisses. In the end, the second group of sisters also walked out of church and they were also upset with me. I remained firm in my belief that the sacred child was nothing more than a statue — and one that was slobbered over, too. Who in the world ever said the cold plaster child was a holy object of the Church? Who? I couldn't figure that out.

...

Today as an adult, I still say my silent prayers and I still feel that comforting presence that is there with me. No one can tell me any different about this. As a child, I knew what I felt. I understood though that this was not a magical remedy to my troubles. It was going to take a life time and a lot of hard work and soul searching if I was ever going to survive growing up.

I do not begrudge my childhood experiences nor do I hold any anger or hate towards my father. I miss and love him even though as a child I didn't. Now I can readily see that all my childhood problems, negative and hurtful, were, in reality, life changing experiences that were meant to teach me how to become a stronger person.

Certainly a six-year-old can't think such thoughts; the best I could do was feel the need to be myself, even if I didn't know exactly who that person called Me really was. Today, I am a blessed man. Back then, I was blessed too. But I didn't know it.

A Hole Is To Dig

One hot stuffy Saturday afternoon, when I was quite young, my brother Fred and I were standing, side by side, on the north side of our property, peering towards our neighbor's house through the cracks in the fence.

Suddenly Fred felt a hard blow on the left side of his face. I saw dust flying all around us and some of the small pieces of mud stung my face as well.

Fred let out a scream of pain.

Neither of us knew why our Father, after seeing us peeking through the fence-crack, came outside, picked up a grapefruit-sized ball of hard mud full of small rocks, and threw it at us.

Fred, who was taller than I was, was an easier target. Plus he was closer to the direction from where this ball of mud, rocks and anger came from. Why did dad do this? We still don't know. But luckily, it didn't leave a scar on Fred's face, even though the memory of that day is permanently etched in his mind.

I suppose you can always look at something positively, regardless of whether it's hurtful at the time. We had to be tough to survive with all the intimidation at home and on the street. We had to stand up for ourselves and take whatever came our way, good or bad, or in between.

There were so many bullies in our neighborhood, and we never knew when they were going to attack us. I guess, in that way, dad was our proving ground, our training camp for abuse and bullies.

There was a kid named Florian who was always picking on me. He was older and stronger than I. Most everyone was. Well, on this day, Fred and I were out in the back yard pulling and raking up weeds, rocks and other trash – we always had tasks set up by our father to keep us busy or to merely punish us. So Fred says to me – "Hey Joseph, look who's walking across the street, Florian, that guy that's always beating you up."

Right then, Fred became my manager, coach and personal trainer. He said, "Joseph, I want you to beat the shit out of Florian." I was five at the time and wouldn't have challenged Florian on my own. But in this case, I had my older brother with me. He was my *vaque*, my support, and that was all I needed.

Fred gave me some quick assessments on how to handle the situation. "I want you to teach this guy a lesson so that he doesn't ever bother you again. Now, when Florian swings at you, duck, then hit him as hard as you can in the stomach. Really hard," Fred said.

So we walked over and stopped Florian.

I stood right in front of him and shouted, "Why are you always beating me up?"

Florian looked at me, with a puzzled look,— took a swing and I ducked under it. Following Fred's advice, I closed my fist, swung as hard as I could into the middle of Florian's stomach. This doubled him over. He crumpled, holding his mid-section and moaning.

Fred and I walked off and that was when I acquired a certain strut to my walk. One that said, *Don't you ever mess with me again.* Florian never bothered me after that. So Fred's counsel worked.

Once every couple of years, Fred and I were assigned a really important job by our father. Not only important to him, but to everyone in the family. This was the digging of a new hole for the family throne, the indispensable outhouse.

This wasn't just any hole. We didn't have engineer's specs for the job, but after years of digging holes, we knew it had to measure up properly or the throne would be too large, or possibly too small for the size of the hole. It had to be just right. If not, it could fall through with someone in it. Most likely me. Hey!—-Maybe,— dad.

As I remember, the hole had to be five feet square, and about six feet deep. To be on the safe side, Fred and I dug it down eight feet. We figured, the deeper the hole, the more time to fill it up. Of course, each hole was in a different spot in the yard. Don't ask me how we remembered where the last spot was, we just knew. Some days we actually had fun doing this. Weekdays, after school, you'd often see us digging. We had a time limit on this project – for obvious reasons.

Starting off was kind of easy because the dirt was soft on top. We took turns with the pick and shovel. However, as the hole got deeper, the job got tougher. Especially for me.

At first, you could see our whole body. Then we were waist deep, and you could see only half of us. Digging, we flung the shovel full of dirt over our shoulder, making sure to get it far enough away from the edge of the hole so it wouldn't fall back in.

As the hole got deeper, it got harder to remove the dirt. Being short didn't help. Soon it was really hard for me to pitch the dirt upward and away from the hole. It often fell back on top of me. When I got tired of the dirt going down my neck, we'd switch tools. I'd give the shovel to Fred; he'd give me the pick. I don't know which one was the harder job. It was like we were both sentenced to a chain gang.

When we got down past four feet, it was torture. After all, Fred and I were shorter than four feet ourselves. At five feet we brought out the five gallon buckets and ropes.

We would fill a bucket with dirt, and the kid outside the hole pulled the bucket up and emptied it. I wasn't strong enough to haul dirt, so I stayed with the hole-digging and bucket-filling.

Once in a while, some of our friends helped out. We hung around with Tony Martinez and his brothers, Carlos and Herman, and they were our main helpers. (By the way, Tony still holds the record for the longest incumbent mayor of Las Vegas, but unless I'm mistaken, his excavation skills didn't have anything to do with his mayoral success).

The greatest challenge came, when, at the end of the day, one of us (me) had to crawl out of the hole. Eight feet down, this wasn't that easy. But we were also well trained in doing this part of the job and quite proficient at doing so. I know this story by now may seem quite long, but you have to realize, it was a deep hole we'd gotten ourselves into, and the work was, well, both timely and critical to the family.

Anyway, once we were done digging, there was still more work to do. Now came the job of moving the piled-up dirt to the old outhouse hole, and topping it off. Once this was done, now we had to move the outhouse to its new location. We used steel bars and round posts to roll the wooden outhouse — a foot or two at a time — toward the freshly dug hole. This, too, was very hard work. Even Dad helped out,— sometimes.

That night, Fred and I slept well. Maybe we dreamed of digging, maybe we didn't. But at least we knew, even in our sleep, that we wouldn't have to dig again for another year.

As a boy, I always wished we had a nice fence in the front of the house. One day, Fred and I decided to build one. Of course we had no materials, only a couple of hammers and a hand saw. Our cousin, Nash Lucero, a local contractor, was building houses on the corner of Valencia Street and New Mexico Avenue. *This by the way, was the former location of the Christian Brother's School.* After dark, Fred and I rolled a wheelbarrow to the site and got all the wood we needed for our fence.

After many nights we had enough materials to construct the fence. First, we dug the holes for the posts. Then we set each post in its designated spot, and tamped it down tight with extra dirt.

We nailed the lattice, one piece at a time, and did a pretty good job for kids; I guess Fred was twelve and I was ten. Anyway, we finished building the fence which included a gate and then we painted it green and we were proud of our artistry.

A couple months went by and one day, we noticed the fence was torn down. Some sections were lying flat on the ground. Others were twisted and hanging to a corner post. It looked like a mean dust devil had done its worst.

Later, we found out that our father had knocked the fence down and torn it apart so it couldn't be repaired.

He'd destroyed all of our handiwork — and for no apparent reason.

But more than that, he'd knocked our spirits deeper into the dirt. But I suppose that's where he wanted us to stay.

Chief Pontiac

You wouldn't think a fence, a simple structure made of wood, would last so long in someone's memory. But when I think back, I came to understand the fence was literally destroyed by a whirlwind. Not the type unleashed by the indomitable power of mother nature, but by the cruel intention of human nature.

In this case, it was the whirlwind of my father's anger which he directed at the fence. In the end, better to rage against a fence than the two young boys that built it. Although, looking back, the boys were the ones most affected by my father's fury.

We never knew when the whirlwind was going to spin. Anything, any little thing, might set it off. Could be he woke in a bad mood, maybe feeling hung over from the night before. Sometimes, there was no reason for his rage. Certainly none that a child would understand.

In any event, he obviously had no control over his temper.

I remember one dark, rainy cold night, when one of his meanest moods showed up.

I was ten years old, already in bed and fast asleep, when I felt a strong hand grab my right arm. This was followed by a thunderous voice commanding me to get up. It was Wille, my father. Such an unbecoming name for this larger-than-life, bigger-than-anger man — or so it seems to me now. Wille sounds like someone you might be friends with, but not so, ever, with *this* Wille.

As I said, it was a stormy night and the wind had forced the front gate open on the fence. The wind was slamming it back and forth, open and shut, back and forth, and this made my father crazy. He forced me out of bed, half asleep. I didn't have time to get properly dressed. Out the back door he pushed me, wearing only a pair of jeans. No shoes or socks, no shirt or jacket. Just me and my jeans.

The ice cold rain drops woke me up in a hurry. They pummeled my bare thin torso, and it felt like I was getting hit with hailstones. Maybe I was.

I figured it would only take me three minutes to run to the front yard, close the gate, run back, hop into bed, pull up the warm covers and go back to sleep. Boy, did I have that wrong.

I closed the gate, latched shut. Then, as I hurried to the back door, getting nailed by the rain, I heard my father yelling. This was followed by my mother's screams.

Suddenly, I was met by my mother. She was running in the rain and she clasped my arm forcefully and swung me around in the opposite direction. "Run," she hollered. *"Corre, Corre."*

We took off as fast as we could and I felt sharp pebbles on my bare wet feet. At that time none of the neighborhood roads were paved. They were just plain dirt roads and on this night it was also a very muddy dirt road.

My mother ran faster than I'd ever seen her run before — out the driveway, down West National Avenue to the next block at the corner of New Mexico Avenue. We ran past the San Miguel Court House, zoomed right past Our Lady of Sorrows Catholic Church. (*Sorry Lord, no time now to stop and pray and kiss baby Jesus*)

By this time we were soaking wet, cold and muddy, but we kept on running. At last we came to the place where I usually went when I ran away, or when I was chased from home — The Historic Plaza Park. We ran until we reached the outside entrance of the Romero Building.

Picture this. It's raining hard, and very windy, and it's now past midnight and my mother is in a rain-soaked cotton dress and slippers and I am just wearing wet pants and no shirt or shoes and we're both hugging each other to keep warm under the protection of the little cubby hole entrance of the Romero building.

What to do? We don't know.

We are both scared, knowing that my father is coming after us. What would he do? We didn't know. How could he hurt us more than this?

We'll find out soon enough, he's coming.

But if Wille *was* coming, we knew what to watch for. A light green 1951 Pontiac Chieftain. The name of the car came from an Indian chief named Pontiac and the hood was adorned with the likeness of this great warrior. Imagine an

Indian head that glowed at night with the reflection of the night sky or the lights of cars or even the imagination of a boy. Well,— you get the picture.

When Wille was out drinking, or perhaps coming back from working in Santa Fe, we'd keep watch from the living room window for the glowing hood ornament. We had a clear view of West National Avenue all the way down to the corner of the Plaza.

At home, we'd taught ourselves to spot Wille's car from a far distance. *The glowing Chieftain head was like a living monument flying through the darkness.* And when we spotted it, this gave us plenty of time to get undressed, jump into bed, and pretend to be asleep. All the time hoping he wouldn't start fighting with Mother.

So there we were – Mother and I – huddled in front of the Romero building. We kept our eyes in the direction of our house, which was two and a half city blocks away, and we watched for the *glowing Chieftain.*

Once in a while we'd look off to the left, thinking he might come from South Gonzales Street.

What should we do? Stand there all night?

We had nowhere to go; we were chilled to the bone.

"*Joseph, ahi vine el Wille!* There he comes!" My mother gasped.

She was right. There was the 1951 Pontiac.

And in front of it, the *glowing Chieftain.*

We froze like rabbits. She took my hand, and hers was really cold.

What should we do? Run, stay? And If we run – where to?

The green Pontiac slowly rounded the corner of West National and Hot Springs.

We kept our eyes focused on the Chief's head as the green car made the gradual turn around the south side of the park. We were so afraid, that we gave up on an escape plan.

So there we were – caught. Held prisoners in front of the Romero building. Afraid of the night, the Chief, Wille, the cold rain, all manner of unknown things. Mostly it was the unknown that kept us prisoner. Frozen with fear, we waited.

I don't believe my mother and I said a single word to each other all this time. We were just dreading the moment when the green Pontiac with the *glowing Chieftain* would stop, the driver's door would fling open and the voice of wrath from within – "*Get in the fucking car!*"

Then the dreaded moment came.

The car stopped.

Time stopped.

The driver's door slowly opened.

My Mother and I very quietly started crying. We didn't want to show our fear. We wanted to be strong for each other.

Then, to our surprise, we were blinded by a spot light mounted on the fender of the car.

His car doesn't have a spot light? I thought to myself.

But this is a green 1951 Pontiac Chieftain with a glowing American Indian hood ornament!

A black figure of a man slid out of the driver's seat, stood up straight and tall next to the car.

Wille? Mother called out.

The man walked towards us. When he was about three feet away, he said, "Mrs. Baca? Is that you? What are you doing out here? Who's that with you?"

The man was Mr. James Baca, our neighbor on Valencia Street, one block from our place.

Mr. Baca was a police officer for the town of Las Vegas. *"Why are you both here soaking wet at one o'clock in the morning?"* he asked.

We told him the sad story. But he already knew who we were and who my father was and he was aware of what can happen on a cold dark night when someone's being chased by a madman. He helped us into his car and took us somewhere, but to this day, I can't remember exactly where it was or what it looked like because the memory's all gone with the terror of that night.

In those days, the Police Department was on such a small budget, they couldn't afford police cars for their officers. So they had to use their personal cars to conduct patrols around town.

Officer Baca had the exact same car as Wille did. A 1951 green Pontiac Chieftain, complete with glowing hood ornament.

Today, over sixty years later, whenever I walk or drive past the Romero Building, I glance over at the front entrance of that building, and see – day or night – a scared woman and a frightened little boy. I can see them there, shivering. It's always a dark, cold wet night in that small cubicle and in my mind's eye, there's always a ghostly Chieftain tracing a path around the Plaza.

Once, at only ten years old, I tried to conquer my fear of the Chieftain with the glowing hood ornament. It was another rainy night and father invited mom to go with him to the neighborhood liquor store known as Oliva's Liquor Store on New Mexico Avenue. I didn't want mom to go alone with dad. I was afraid that if there was an accident, she may die alone. I wanted to die with her. Dad walked into Oliva's and stayed for what seemed like hours talking to others buying their bottle of spirits. It started raining very hard as mom and I sat in the car. We really wanted to go home. I then decided to take charge. I got out of the car on the passenger side, walked around the front, and sat on the driver's seat. I was determined to take us home.

That plan didn't work. As I soon found out. Dad finally approached the car and didn't say a word when he found me behind the wheel of the Chieftain. He just gave the order; *andle, vamos. My tiny hand on the key, foot on the gas pedal,* which I could only reach by scooting down on the seat. Lucky for me, his car was automatic, I started the engine and took off heading South on New Mexico Avenue. As I approached the intersection of West National, I signaled to turn right. I felt relieved because we were just one block away from home heading west.

Then, before I could turn, I heard the command; no, para donde vas!!!! dale derecho. Father directed me to drive on and head out of town.

As I say, I was only ten. Too small to see over the steering wheel so I slanted my head forward, pushed my eyes up ward so I could see the road in between the steering wheel and the dash board. Remember, this is a time when there was no I-25 going to Santa Fe, only the narrow two lane old Las Vegas Highway.

I didn't know how far out we were headed, but I was determined to turn around and head back home once we reached Romeroville, New Mexico, which is about ten miles from Las Vegas. Mom was very quiet as she pretended to listen to dad's gibberish conversation, in between his gulping sound as he drank from his whisky bottle. I was quiet as a scared mouse, especially when I saw the bright lights of a large tractor trailer rig approaching. The road was only wide enough to handle two cars, much less a car and a large semi truck.

All I could hear was the deafening sound of the rain pouring down on the hood and the roof top and the slushy, swish- - - swish- - - swish- - - of the windshield wipers. Then suddenly, I felt the car being pushed to the side of the wet slippery road as a semi truck zoomed by.

Finally, Romeroville. I slowed down, looking for a spot to turn around, brought the car to a jerking sudden stop. When it was clear, I slowly turned around and we headed home.

Blessings in Disguise

I bless the memory of my mother.
Margaret Martha Griego Baca
Born: August 9, 1916
Died: June 14, 1983.

Mother had been ill, battling cancer for over ten years. She had grown tired of medical treatment, doctors, and in the end, wanted nothing to do with hospitals. She had been living in California, but by the time I moved my family back to New Mexico, *latter part of 79*, she was living in her own apartment and worked at Furr's Cafeteria, where she had many friends. I used to enjoy visiting her at her apartment where we sat and talked. Interestingly, many times our conversations centered around old memories of running away from Wille and the fun games we shared when he wasn't home. Laughter filled her apartment.

Eventually, her illness wore her out and she became too weak to continue working and could no longer live alone, so mom moved in with Elizabeth, the jokester of the family, who lived in Albuquerque. In fact, most of my brothers and sisters lived in the Albuquerque area at the time, except for Jeannette, Ereasmo and I, we lived in Las Vegas. Jessy and his family, I believe, lived in Los Lunas, New Mexico.

As time wore on, we all knew mothers' time was coming and she knew it as well. One weekend Jeannette and I drove to Albuquerque to visit her at Elizabeth's home. All the kids were in the living room visiting with our dear mother and with each other. Conversation and light laughter filled the livingroom as mom sat on the couch with others sitting on either side. Loretta and I were sitting on chairs facing mom at a distance of about three feet. I kept looking at mom as she kept her eyes fixed it seemed, on a corner of the ceiling. I could see a far away look in her eyes as if she was concentrating on something in the far distance past the ceiling and into the blue heavens.

Even though there was talking and commotion in the room, I could sense a strong spirit of deep silence and contemplation around my mom. I stood up and walked up to her and knelt at her feet. While holding her hands in mine I softly asked, *What are you thinking mom? En que piensa mama? What are you feeling? Que es lo que sentis?*

Tengo miedo. I'm afraid.
Miedo de que mama? Fear of what mother?
I feel sad and guilty.
Why guilty mom?
I feel guilty because I feel I am abandoning my kids and leaving all of you behind.
WOW!!!!——

After all her suffering she went through, all the physical, verbal, and spiritual abuse, and even while standing at death's doorway, our dear mother was worried about her kids. Feeling sad and guilty because she believed she was abandoning us.

To the readers, this reveals the type of precious person our mother was. The strong spirit she really was while on this earth.

No mom, you have nothing to feel sad or guilty about, I told her, kneeling at her feet and caressing her hands. We looked into each others eyes, and possibly beyond that, and I said, mom you took very good care of your husband and all your children. Look at all that you did for us. You always protected, and loved us. You are a very strong person and should be proud of who you are and what you have accomplished. Don't feel guilty mom. You have always been a very loving mother to your kids. I love you very much mother.

I just stayed kneeling at her feet and didn't know what else to share with her because I didn't want to cry in her presence. Though we both saw the tears swelling up in our eyes. I felt a huge lump in my throat, but I wanted to be strong for her sake.

Finally we helped her onto a wheel chair and we all went out on the front yard to get some New Mexico sunshine and fresh air. Then, so quickly it seemed, it was late afternoon and Jeannette and I had to return to Las Vegas and back to work the next day.

As we walked away, I turned around and looked straight into my mother's brown, but sad eyes. With a smile, I waved to her as I said good-by. Next day, (Monday), Jeannette and I got a call.

You guys better hurry up and come back to Albuquerque, Mama is not looking good at all and has gotten worse over night.

By the time we got to Elizabeth's house, our lovely mother had left us.

She passed away peacefully in one of the bedrooms where she had been sleeping and the family waited before calling the ambulance so that Jeannette and I could say our final good-by. We both knelt at her bed side and cried and said a prayer.

Next time we saw our mother, was at the mortuary where she was being prepared and being cared for. We asked the mortician if the entire group of children could go inside and view her as she was being prepared. At first he didn't know how to respond.

That is a very unusual request and something that is normally not allowed or done.

We waited quietly.

Well, ok ——— I'll allow you to see her.

We all walked into the room where our mother was and took one last look at the beautiful angel who had always been there to protect us as children, and as adults.

After her burial, Fred and I went to her apartment and just sat in the car and recalled fond memories of our mother, at which time, Fred stated it perfectly:

If there was ever an angel on earth,- ~ ~ ~ it was our mother.

Fred also said to me: *That day as you walked away from mom and you looked back to wave good-by to her, you knew didn't you?*

I could see it in your eyes. You knew that would be the last time you would see her alive.

To this day, I miss my mother dearly. But I know she is happy, safe and not suffering any more.

When The Cat's Away The Mice Will Play

My sister Elizabeth was good at playing tricks, and somehow she got away with it. One time I fell asleep at the kitchen table and my mouth was open, as I snored loudly. Along comes Elizabeth with a pair of my dirty socks and she stuffs one of them into my mouth.

As you might imagine, that really woke me up in a hurry. But I was mad!

Everyone — my mom and the others, including of course Liz — were all laughing at me, so it was hard to be angry with the whole family carrying on like this.

Liz once did this same thing — only with *red hot chili* — not to me but to one of the other kids. You might think this was a killer prank, and maybe it was, but, remember, it's New Mexico, and chili, no matter how hot, is something you can always live with. Maybe I should also add — as long as you're a native New Mexican and have been eating the stuff all your life

One night, when Wille was away somewhere, we decided to have our own little fun parade right there in the kitchen. As a child, did you ever do this? We cut up a lot of paper into very small pieces.

We all pitched in to get this playful project done. We cut and tore up piles of paper from magazines, paper bags, newspapers, most likely *the Daily Optic. Back when it was daily,* and even white writing paper. You name it, it was in there, and our laughter filled the kitchen as we got more and more excited.

Finally we'd cut up enough paper for the big event — a crazy paper confetti party. Remember though, Wille wasn't at home, so we all went a little nuts with this thing. The idea being, when we had enough little bits of paper, we'd create a fiesta of flying confetti. A snowfall celebration of something, well, we couldn't even explain it if we wanted to — even now. Except — when the cat's away the mice will play!

To put it another way, we were free to be ourselves.

Maybe not for long. But for a little while anyway.

Mom helped us to fill up a big sack with the cut up paper.

Then we formed a circle in the kitchen and we all dug our hands into the sack and laughed and cheered and made it snow in the kitchen.

At the same time we jostled each other around as we went for more and more grabs of confetti. It was wonderful to see and hear Mom laughing and acting like a little kid throwing confetti with such abandon and just being happy. I don't remember ever seeing her so joyous in my life.

And soon the kitchen floor was deep white.

Bits of paper littered the table, the stove and the dishes. We looked like snow babies as well, with big flakes stuck to our hair and decorating our shoulders.

And then – like a demon in the dark . . .

The glowing hood ornament appeared.

Fred peeked out the window, and saw it first.

The 1951 Pontiac Chieftain, slowly crunching up to the house.

The cheers of joy that had, moments before, filled the kitchen, now turned to shrieks of desperation. We knew we had to have the place spotless in a matter of seconds. But was it even possible?

No one knew what Wille would do since we'd never done anything like this before.

Mom grabbed the broom and wildly swept the little-bitty papers into small piles. The rest of us dropped down on hands and knees and scooped it up as fast as we could. Some of us used a towel to wipe papers off the top of the stove and the kitchen table.

"*Apurate, andale, apurate – hurry-hurry!*" Mom called out as the Pontiac head-lights came across the side of the house.

He was driving very slowly.

This was of course because he'd been drinking.

The Pontiac came up to the side of the house and for a moment,— the engine growled softly, then softened and was still. The driver's door creaked open.

But our luck stayed with us on this crazy night. By the time Wille opened the kitchen door, the kitchen was clean and we'd already scrambled like mice into the little bedroom where we all slept. Then we held our breath. One piece of paper – just one! – could cause a terrible uproar.

We waited, holding our breath.

But our luck held.

For some reason, Wille was in a happy mood, and he didn't make a fuss over anything.

That's one night I'll never forget — the joy, the explosive release of tension, my mother's face, the fun, the laughter, the furor of cleaning up the mess before the boom fell, and then the silence afterwards as the mice lay quietly in their beds.

Of course, like many poor families in those days, we didn't have many fancy toys to play with, so we invented our own. There was the *tire ride.* We had several old car and truck tires sitting around the yard. Our back yard was pretty large and had an uphill grade to it. We'd get a big tire, roll it up the hill, then we'd curl one of the kids into the tire, and roll it down the hill while running alongside, laughing hysterically.

One time Fred and I squeezed little Liz inside the tire, got it to the top of the hill and — *let go.* Liz screamed out loud as the tire picked up more speed than we expected. The tire got away from us, we couldn't catch up with it. Straight down the hill it rolled until it slammed against the west wall of the house. The tire hit so hard that the force of the blow spat Liz out into the dirt. Then the tire banged on its side with a big *whump.*

Liz was really shaken up.

I felt okay though because Liz was the one who stuffed the dirty sock in my mouth.

All's fair in love and war, right?

My sisters had it pretty rough later on when it came to going out on dates. They didn't get to be like other young ladies who had friends and dated regularly. The thought of bringing a boyfriend to the house to introduce to our dad was out of the question. I really can't remember any of my sisters going to a school dance or even the yearly prom. Maybe they did, and I was just too young to remember it but I really don't think it happened at all. Speaking of dancing, my sisters were the ones that taught me how to dance the jitterbug. Yap, right there in the living room floor when their school girl friends came to visit. Of course, you know this only happened when Wille wasn't home.

There was one time when some guys drove past our house and slowed down hoping to see my sisters to flirt with them. At the same time, Tony Martinez and his brothers had come to see Fred and me. They were in the house and the would-be suitors were outside the house.

Wille was working in Santa Fe, so Tony, Fred and I decided to play a prank on the boys. We'd imitate Wille and scare the guys away. One of Tony's brothers put on a top coat and hat and Fred got Wille's twenty-two rifle.

It was around dusk and the shadows were stretching way out under the cottonwood trees. The hopeful guys made many passes in their car. They went up and down the street and called out the sister's names. There was much whistling and some off-key singing.

Pretty soon it was sundown, and dark.

We went out on the front porch and waited for the Casanovas to return.

Here they came again, revving their engine, and whistling. The car slowed down, the guys called for the girls. "Come on girls, let's go for a ride. *Andale* Juliette, Elizabeth, Theresa, I want to kiss you. We'll bring you back soon."

Then *Carlos*, the tallest of the Martinez brothers, dressed up in the big overcoat, hat and carrying *wild Willie's* rifle, came out from behind a pillar on the porch, and shouted, *Que quieren aqui, cabrones. Se me van o los mato!* ("What do you want here, bastards, get out of here or I'll kill you.")

Wille's likeness, his perfectly disguised double, raised the rifle to his shoulder, aimed it directly at the Casanovas, who immediately ducked down, rolled up their windows, and drove away as fast as they could.

You should have heard us laughing after they left.

Even the sisters joined in too.

On another occasion, Wille was working out of town in Santa Fe, so the girls went to see a movie at the Kiva Theater. I feel it's only fair to add that Wille didn't go to Santa Fe to get drunk. For all his faults, he was a hard worker and a good tailor, a profession he learned from his mother, who was a seamstress with her own business.

Anyway, Mom gave the sisters permission to go to the movies, but with strict orders to be home by ten o'clock that night. Jeannette, Elizabeth, Juliette, and Theresa got all dolled up for their big night out. Fred and I sensed that Mom was nervous about her decision to let the sisters leave but she'd already said yes and the girls were well on their way down West National Avenue. Meanwhile, the hours seemed to drag on and we could feel the tension building as mother watched the clock.

Finally the clock struck ten and the sisters were not home. Mom was getting really worried. Fred and I followed her every move as she paced by the front door, gazed down National Avenue, with no sign of the sisters, then we followed her to the back door in hopes of seeing them. This was the routine for the next hour and a half.

Between trips from the front door to the back door, Mom talked to herself, and I vividly remember her words: *Que fregaditas esas muchachitas que no llegan. Ya es pasado las once de la noche. Onde andarán? Fred, Joseph, que vamos a ser?* Which is to say, "how dare these little girls. Why won't they come home? It's already past eleven at night! Where could they be? Fred – Joseph – what are we going to do?"

Mom vowed never to let them go out again. But her main worry was, of course, El Wille. What if he came home all of a sudden and found the girls weren't there?

Man, all the demons from hell would be let loose if this happened, and our mother would have to pay the fiddler and take all the blame and God knows what humiliations would come her way, and ours as well.

Fred and I decided to take charge of the situation. We came up with a way to teach the *fregaditas, these little brats,* a lesson they'd never forget. Our plan required materials, ingenuity and creativity. But hey, that's how we learned to live, grow up, survive.

What we decided to do was along the same lines as how we dispersed the casanovas, only this time, we'd construct a demon from hell that would greet the girls when they returned. *La Llorona,* the witch of Northern New Mexico was about to pay my sisters a special visit.

First, we got a broom, then ran a piece of heavy wire across the bristles, added a piece of wood trim for support, placed a paper bag over the broom, painted big red evil eyes and added a satanic mouth with huge white fangs dripping with blood.

To make the demon look larger and more threatening, we gave it a black top coat and added a hat with a large rim, tilted to one side so as to hide one of the demon's evil eyes. Mom figured out what Fred and I were planning for the girls and she slowly started giggling with us as we gave life to our demon of the night. We could tell this was helping to ease the fear Mom was feeling.

We knew the girls would come into the house through the back door because that was the route all of us kids normally took. So we propped the demon outside between the back door and the screen door, and waited for the fregaditas.

By now, it was nearly midnight. Mom was both angry and scared, but mostly, I guess, worried.

As for Fred and me, well, we were savoring the moment. We knew the power of what we'd created, and from a slight distance and the right amount of moonlight, our demon looked scary, to say the least.

So we waited . . .

We could hear Mom talking to herself in the kitchen. She was pacing again. "Where are the girls? What if they were kidnapped? What if they're hurt and can't get home?" The more Mom fretted the more Fred and I bit our tongues to keep from laughing – not at Mom's distress – but at what we knew was about to happen the moment the fregaditas showed up.

That hellfire demon was going to frighten our sisters right out of their petticoats and bobby socks. The *fregaditas* were going to learn a life-lesson from their diabolical brothers.

Well, finally,—the big moment arrived.

Mom exclaimed: "*Ahí vienen las fregaditas. Al fin. Que fragadas.* There they come, finally, those little brats.

To Fred and I, this moment was pay day. We could hardly contain ourselves, and while mom was wringing her hands, we were biting our knuckles to keep from laughing at the whole preposterous event that was about to take place.

There was the demon.

And there were the naughty girls in their fluffed-out dresses.

The night held so many secrets.

And a new one was about to unfold.

Maybe from sheer relief at seeing the girls coming, Mom started to crack up.

And there she was, all of a sudden, enjoying our prank along with us.

As we peeked through the backdoor curtain, the girls came forward out of the darkness, whispering to one another.

They were at the steps, kind of huddling together for moral support. *As if that were going to help them.* As they stood right in front of the screen door, Juliette, the second eldest, reached for the door handle, opened the screen door which made a lonely creaking sound – then she stopped in her tracks. *Ohhi—mira lo que esta ahi!* – Look what's there!

The demon from Hell dripped fang-blood and leered.

The girls screamed

Holding tight to each other, they backed away from the door, one step at a time.

And then, like deer before the gun, they turned and ran in the same direction.

Fred and I watched in astonishment as our sisters ran blindly towards the family throne.

By then, Mom, Fred and I were in hysterics.

For, it was obvious now, the girls really believed they were running from a demon at the door. Maybe – *La llorona* – *o undemonio del infernio.* The faceless woman of legend who was also a demon from hell.

All four sisters piled into the small outhouse and closed the door.
Mom, Fred and I roared with laughter. Such a moment only comes but once in a life time. We laughed our hearts out.

Moments later, a big neighborhood dog showed up, and went around the yard sniffing until it came up to the outhouse.

When the dog heard strange noises inside, it started growling and the girls, thinking that the dog was the demon, screamed some more.

All this time, Mom, Fred and I are roaring with laughter as the dog circled the outhouse, sniffing and grunting like a pig.

We could easily imagine the *fregaditas* shivering in the outhouse as they imagined some kind of demonic ritual going on before the devilish one gathered them up to take them to his den.

By now, it is way past midnight.

Our merriment was about done.

Time to free the sisters from their five-by-five stink prison.

But I, being the youngest and mischievous one, thought we should leave them in there a little longer.

However, even when we all went to the outhouse to talk to the girls and convince them to come out and get inside the house, it didn't work. I told them that it was all a trick. I assured them that what they saw was no demon, evil spirit, or La Llorona.

But this didn't work either.

The ladies were not coming out.

"Hey," I said, "the noise you heard – that sniffing around the outhouse, well it was a big dog."

Silence.————————-.

I told them,

"You know, Fred and I made that demon and put him between the screen door and the back door to frighten you. It was all a joke."

Silence.————————.

"It was all to teach you a lesson for coming home so late," Fred added.

Silence.————————.

We stayed out until 2: a. m. trying to convince them, but our pleas had no effect.

At last, we went inside, and much later, one by one, the girls tiptoed into the house.

And we all went to bed.

Lucky for us, all this happened while El Wille was in Santa Fe. He may have liked the demon trick, but as for the girls, if Wille had been home, they'd have met a real hellfire demon.

After that night, life went on normally in the Baca house.

Well, as normal as could be expected in such a place and such a time, and with such a father. Present or not, his spirit was always there, and I suppose, it still is.

The unexplainable

We had just given our sisters the scare of their life. Perhaps it was my turn to be scared out of my britches. One night I saw something that to this day I can not explain. After watching TV at the Herrera home, I started walking home at about 11:45 p. m. It was very dark and windy as the branches from trees swayed back and forth and bent sideways by the force of the howling winds. Lopez Street where the Herrera's lived, is a very narrow street with only room for one car at a time. I had walked the length of about two homes, when at a distance, I saw what appeared to be three glowing balls of fire. They weren't actually burning balls of fire, because there were no flames involved. Rather, they glowed with the mix of bright red and orange which seemed to vibrate out of them.

I finally reached the spot where they lay among the weeds as if hovering about three inches above the ground. I felt confused, scared and very inquisitive as to what these glowing balls were and why they were there in this dark alley. Though I was scared, I also felt a strong urge to walk closer to them, and I did, to about a distance of five feet, then I thought, *"What would happen if I reached out and touched them"?*

I rubbed and wiped my eyes and even pinched my arm thinking I could be dreaming. But then, I heard Corrine, one of the Herrera daughters come out onto their front yard as she called out to her mother, *"donde esta el cajete, mama"?* She was looking for their tin tub outside. I quickly thought of calling her and asking her to come to where I was to see if she too saw what I was seeing. But then she quickly went inside her house and I did not call to her. I could have gone to her house but didn't think of it. I guess these glowing balls of light were meant for my eyes only.

I wondered if I should walk or run past these strange things very quickly so I could get home. Instead, my fear was stronger than my inquisitive mind and I decided to turn around, circle the entire block and hurriedly walked home. It was past midnight by the time I got home. Opening the kitchen back door and walking across our tattle tale old kitchen floor was a big challenge. More about what this means later on.

Next morning I told my Mother what I had seen. She in turn told my father to which he said, "it's the devil. Es el Diablo. The devil is after him because Joseph hasn't been going to church."

I quietly thought, "neither has he, why doesn't the devil appear to him?" I never saw the glowing balls of fire again. I sometimes find myself hoping I will, some dark, windy night.

Uncle Joe and Aunt Esther

My Mother had one brother. His name was Joe and he was married to Esther. They had no children but they wanted one very badly. I remember one time they wanted to adopt my sister Elizabeth. First it was my chance, later it would be hers to move in with them. All I know is, they wanted to adopt me. Uncle Joe asked me to move-in with them for a year – so I did.

That was in 1954 and I was a fourth grade student at the old North Public School building in Las Vegas, New Mexico. Today that school is called Don Cecilio Elementary.

I was eight, and in one way, I was a happy little boy living with my uncle and aunt – for the first time, I had my own bedroom, my own warm bed, and I remember jumping on the bed out of sheer pleasure of having such a thing. I'd smell the clean fresh bed sheets and the plump pillow. Then I'd go into my very own bathroom, which was but seven feet away from my very own bed. The luxury! The unbelievable, thrilling, heart-breaking luxury of this cannot even be explained, leastwise, by me.

Another exciting experience I enjoyed living with my uncle and aunt was,— dinner at Estellas Restaurant every Friday night. I could have anything I desired on the menu and as much as this little boy wanted.

Picnics were a semi-regular event as well. One time the Gonzales family joined us on a picnic up to Gallinas. My uncle asked Alfred, one of the Gonzales' sons and me to go fetch a watermelon from the river where it was placed to keep it cool. There we were, Alfred and I, legs spread and planted firmly on flat rocks on the river. I bent down to lift the melon, my feel slid from under me and fell flat into the cold water. I got scared, screamed, then Alfred pulled me and the melon out to safety. As we arrived back at the dinner table, soaking wet, it was obvious what had happened and loud laughter could be heard coming from everyone at the table. Me,—well,—I was still crying.

My aunt's parents lived in Albuquerque. Quite often my aunt and I traveled to visit her parents. On the way there, I remember we would stop at several of the roadside stands set up by American Indians. There we bought Indian bread, an assortment of vegetables, fruit and once in a while a piece of fine Indian jewelry. I recall one day when visiting my aunt's family, we sat at the table to eat. It was a traditional Spanish meal with beans, tortillas, and all the usual foods that go with a Northern Spanish meal. After a full serving, holding my stomach, I complained that it hurt, to which, Cecilia, one of my aunt's sisters replied, while looking at me with a smile, *"pues come mas pa que se te quite."* Translation: *"well, eat more so the pain will go away".* So I did. I ate more. Followed by more complaining, *"now it hurts even more"*, with a groan in my voice. Once again, this filled the room with laughter. Not mine, but there's.

Photo of me, Aunt Esther, Uncle Joe, and my brother Fred.

At my home with my parents, we only had an old outhouse which was cold in winter and hot in summer and smelly year round. It had in it the usual old Montgomery Ward catalogue and if two of us needed to use the outhouse at the same time . . . well, you get the picture.

At eight, I adored music. Music of all kinds. But especially the singing of Frank Sinatra, Tony Bennett, and a bunch of other popular artists from the 1950s. One of my favorite songs was, *Mr. Sandman* released by The Chordettes in 1954.

I used to lie in my big bed and sing myself to sleep. The verse I loved to sing was — "Mr. Sandman bring me a dream, make it the cutest that I've ever seen."

In the good old days, this was the poetry, harmony and rhyme that fed my own dreams. Those sweet words fit perfectly in my mouth when I sang them softly in my bed at night and they tripped off my lips, and who knows where they went — maybe to the Sandman himself — could be, because I actually sang myself to sleep as I tripped off to the land of dreams.

Uncle Joe and Aunt Esther used to manage the California Clothing Store, a department store on the Southwest corner of Old Town Plaza in Las Vegas. When I moved in with them, one of the first things they did for me was to take me into their store and whatever clothes I liked, as much as I wanted were mine to keep. New pants, shoes, shirts, socks and, most important, a warm jacket for winter. Man, I really felt like a million bucks.

I was fed well, too, and though I was skinny, I started gaining a pound or two. Uncle Joe would place a small metal bowl on my head to cut my hair. I didn't mind, it felt kind of cool. He was caring for me. Most of all, I sensed that he was glad I was there, and that made me feel good.   Aunt Esther used to say, "Joseph, my son, when are you going to start calling me Mother?"

I had no ready answer for her. I don't remember if I ever found one. She was who she was, and I was who I was, and even as an eight-year-old I understood the difference between auntie and mommy.

As happy as I was in my new home, with every thing I wanted or needed, deep down I was still pretty sad because I missed my own mother.

Back in those days, people seldom talked about abuse the way we do today. It wasn't done. It didn't matter if it was verbal, physical, mental or even spiritual abuse, there was no law against it except the obvious moral one, but, as I say, people didn't discuss it. So things got overlooked that shouldn't have been.

Practically speaking, if you did report the abuse — who would you report it *to*?

One time, I did report my father to the local police, but my complaint went into their circular file. In most cases, in a small town like Las Vegas, the police were good friends (and often relatives) with the people who were accused of the abuse. I took a beating from my father when I reported him for hitting my mother, my sister and myself. He hit anyone he pleased in our family any time he wanted to, and we had no choice but to accept our lot in life, like so many others who found themselves in this helpless situation.

So now I was nice and snug in my big private bed, and no one at Uncle Joe's and Aunt Esther's would ever think of raising a hand to hurt me, and there I was thinking — *Maybe, if I stay real quiet, just maybe, I can hear my mom crying when my dad is mistreating her. On a cold clear autumn night you could hear the town breathing. But — if I did hear my mom scream — what then? What could I do? I was only eight.*

I felt guilty about all of this because I really believed I'd forsaken Mom by moving out. I'd left her in that lonely, abusive house where El Wille ran things his way, with an open palm or a closed fist.

It made me miserable to think I'd walked out on my brothers and sisters, too, and that I was safe and they were not.

But, in reality, that's just exactly what I had done.

At noon, I walked to my old house from school which was a distance of about three city blocks. I enjoyed that because I got to see Mom and I got to eat some of her simple but delicious meals. My eyes were always bigger than my stomach when it came to mom's traditional Spanish food. Tortillas, a pot of beans with chicos, fried potatoes, corn bread, green chili from Hatch, New Mexico and always a delicious dessert like a pudding called *natillas*.

With very little, Mom made a great deal because she knew how to cook. And, always, she ate last — whatever was left was hers. That's the way she was. She always made sure her children ate first.

She'd greet me with a great big smile and a warm, strong hug. I don't remember Wille saying anything to me when I came to eat lunch. If we didn't see each other for weeks, he still didn't greet me. We were like a couple of strangers. So, I would eat Mom's wonderful cooking, give her a hug, say goodbye, and hurry back to school for my afternoon classes, after which I went to Uncle Joe's and Esther's, where I knew there'd be no yelling, no harsh words, no hitting.

Nonetheless, I was not really happy inside because I knew what was going on in my own home. Seeing Mom at noon only made me sadder afterward because that meant I had to get used to being away from her and saying goodbye all over again when I came over.

After one year with my aunt and uncle, I went back home. It wasn't that I didn't want to stay with Uncle Joe and Aunt Esther — I did. I really did. But, the truth is, I missed my mom so much, and I worried about her all the time. So, after a year, I went back home even though I knew what I was going back to. With me gone from this happy home, it opened the door for my sister Elizabeth to move in, and she did

No Good Clothes to Wear

After living with Uncle Joe and Esther, I came home and saw my life as it really was, just as it had been before I moved out. For one whole blissful year, I'd lived in a safe environment, I'd worn fine clothes to school, I'd had a kindly house to return to when school was finished for the day, and there was never a doubt in my mind about whether my aunt and uncle loved me.

Back at home, life was the same as it was when I left. My father had it in for us, no matter what we did.

So, no more peace and harmony. No more nice clothes. Now that I was growing so fast, I needed clothes more than ever. But such things came by way of our neighbors, not our father. The neighbors had two sons and their clothes fit us. Every once in a while, we'd get a box of clothing they'd outgrown. If I was lucky, I'd rummage through the box before my brother got home. That way I could pick the best things.

I'd shine up the shoes right away. A good shine, and they'd look brand new. As I grew older and got bigger, I used to walk with a friend of mine to the east-side, the so-called rich side of Las Vegas. The best time for these secret strolls was nighttime. We'd travel down the crushed cinder alleys, and if we saw any nice clothes hanging on the clothes lines, we'd hop the fence or just walk straight into the yard and take them.

We were poor. No one needed to tell us that. We knew.

I wasn't overjoyed about getting clothing this way, but I felt at the time that it was necessary for my survival.

At home, we didn't have the nice things like at Uncle Joe's house. For water, there was a single water pipe that came up through the wooden floor of the pantry where my mom kept our canned goods. Naturally, there was no hot water that came sparkling out of a spigot. If we wanted it, we had to boil it on the woodstove.

The woodstove in the kitchen was both for cooking and warmth. For bathing, we used the old fashioned tub or *cajete*. Mother used it as well to wash clothes.

All the children bathed in the same water, one after the other. For privacy, we hung a blanket in the space behind the stove and the wall.

For a long time, I was the smallest child at home until my smaller brother Ereasmo was born, so I was usually the last one to take a bath. I used to have a lot of fun during this time, because when one of my sisters was taking a bath, I would get some ice cold water in a small pan, somehow climb onto the stove and throw the cold water over the back of the stove and splash my sisters with cold, cold water to which I would hear loud screams and a cuss word or two coming from whichever sister happened to be taking a bath. They usually paid me back when it came time for me to take a bath. It was all in fun.

There were nine children — five sisters and four brothers counting myself. We slept in one bedroom on one large bed, and we were packed in like sardines. The smallest and youngest had to sleep on a big stuffed chair until one of the older kids went to live with a relative.

Before my little brother came along, I was the one who slept on that big stuffed chair. That was my bed for ten years. I curled up and covered myself with a blanket, dug my bare feet in between the arm rest and the cushion, rested my head on a pillow and tried to fall asleep. Often that didn't happen, so I lay there listening to the wind prowling around the house, the snores of my siblings, and the barking dogs roaming the neighborhood.

In the morning, it took a while before I could walk because my body was all cramped up from sleeping like a cramped little puppy. But, even so, I remember being thankful for at least having a place to sleep. It wasn't much, but it was something.

* * *

Today, when I look back and remember the past, the hard times, I feel so blessed. What were the hard times for? For this: To teach me to appreciate life.

Yes, I am truly blessed. Today I thank God for the neighbors who gave us clothing to wear.

Sometime ago a war veteran came to my radio station to speak on the show that I host. During the interview I kept looking at him, thinking that I knew him from somewhere. When the mayor, Henry Sanchez, introduced him as Mr. Encinias, I suddenly recognized our guest. Here was one of the brothers that used to give us his outgrown clothing. I reminded him who I was and I told him that he never knew that he was one of my angels. He remembered me and my mother and he said that it made him proud to know that I owned the two original and oldest radio stations in Las Vegas, New Mexico.

I did all I could to hold back my tears during the interview. Seeing Mr. Encinias after so many years touched my heart and brought back so many memories that I am writing about now. Mr. Encinias was a World War II decorated hero who was shot down behind enemy lines and was taken prisoner for many years. Shaking Mr. Encinias hand was yet another blessing. Time circles around and keeps teaching valuable lessons. For me, the learning process is never over. The education continues along.

The Whiskey Drive And The Race For Life

My brother Jessy is the youngest of the boys in my family. He was born March 28, 1958 and I am twelve years older than he is. I don't know why, but when it comes to the three youngest in my family, I have few memories of them growing up. I do have a real hurtful memory regarding Jessy though, and it occurred the night my father allowed Jessy to drink some of his whiskey.

Wille liked to go out for a drive when he was drinking, and he always took Mom with him. On this particular night, Mom had to take Jessy along for the ride because he was too young to be by himself. I came home shortly after they'd left and was already in bed when they arrived.

I remember how it was when they came back from this whiskey drive.

There was something different that cold winter's night – I sensed it the minute they came in the kitchen door.

Wille was laughing. It was a different laugh – a stranger's.

I heard him tell Mama, "*Mira lo. Que brinquideras.* "Look at him– he is jumping a lot." Then came the weird laugh.

I knew what Wille found so amusing. Jessy was drunk. He was going around the house – from the kitchen to dining room, from living room to the couch where Wille and Mom were sitting together.

I listened in bed, keeping my ears open, in case Wille went into one of his sudden unexpected rages. But that wasn't happening. After a little while, I realized I could no longer hear Jessy. Wille was no longer laughing. The house was silent. I listened. There was just the wind rattling the bushes.

Had Jesse fallen asleep? Where was he?

For some reason, a sick feeling came over me. It washed over me like a prickly wave.

The quietness was very strange.

Where was Jesse?

Why was he so quiet?

I couldn't stand it anymore; I put on my pants, shirt and shoes, and crept into the kitchen.

Jesse wasn't there.

Then – for what reason I don't know – I opened the kitchen door and peered into the dark night.

I noticed a movement inside Wille's Pontiac Chieftain.

A shadow moving like a rabbit from the front seat to the back. I walked out and opened the front passenger door to the Pontiac.

There was Jesse, naked but for a pair of undershorts.

He jumped from seat to seat.

It took me but a split second to realize just how drunk he was from Wille's whiskey.

"Jesse," I said, "Come out of there. Let's get inside, come on now."

It took a while to calm him down. He didn't want to stop cavorting, but I got hold of him and hugged him hard. He grew still in the warmth of my arms. Carrying him into the house I felt a sinking feeling like never before in my life. Here was this tiny little body in my arms. His arms and legs dangly, like a rag doll or a puppet.

Tears rolled down my cheeks as I brought him into the house and placed him on the bed where Mom slept. I covered him up and he moaned a little and went to sleep. More than likely, he'd passed out from exhaustion.

Seeing my little brother in this drunken condition made me feel cheap and humiliated and worthless.

I walked into the bedroom where I slept. I now had a bed in one lonely corner. Fred slept in another bed in the opposite corner. I don't recall where the others were, but I know they weren't at home.

I didn't feel like sleeping because there was so much helpless, hopeless anger in me. That was why I didn't consider the consequences of what I was about to do.

I slipped on my heaviest jacket, wiped the tears from my eyes. Then I marched into the dining room where Wille was sitting on the couch drinking. Mom was seated next to him, not because she wanted to but because he had her there where he wanted her and she had no choice but to obey. Her eyes were tired and she looked weary and worn.

I stood face to face with my father, being careful to keep myself a few feet away from him. And then it came out – *my* rage.

"What kind of father are you? Why did you let Jesse get drunk on your nasty whisky? He's just a baby. You could've killed him."

Wille was quiet for a moment. He studied my face.

Then he stood up, picked up a hammer that was on the floor and came after me. If he caught me, I knew he'd strike me dead.

I ran for the kitchen.

Mom jumped in front of Wille and blocked him.

I heard them scuffling as I ran out of the kitchen.

Then I heard him throw her aside, and come clumping after me. The whiskey in him was my advantage. That, and the fact I was younger and faster. All of my instincts kicked in – run for your life because, slow or not, he can find you, especially at night when he can see like a cat.

There was one house where the door was always open for me. The Herrera's. They lived about half a mile away. I ran hard and fast. The moon came out briefly and lit up the bare cottonwood trees. A dog howled. An owl hooted. A siren whined far off somewhere. The wind chased me, but what I feared was El Wille.

I ran without stopping until I came to the Herrera's front door.

I entered the house, clicked the door shut, and locked it.

I was safe.

* * *

Looking back on that night so long ago, I am reminded of the fact that sometimes – even when there was no incident with El Wille – I was forced to sleep outdoors. That was because he'd just locked me out. Then I'd find a sheltered spot somewhere in the back yard and curl up and sleep like a mongrel dog. Many times though, I'd show up at the Herrera home, knowing their door was unlocked just for me. There were times though, mostly during warm summer nights, when I'd sit on a chair out on the porch of the Herrera home, lean it back against the wall and fall asleep. In the morning Mrs. Herrera would open the door and find me sleeping in that chair. She'd scold me gently and ask why I didn't come inside the house. Sometimes I just didn't want to disturb anyone. I wanted to be invisible. If I could've floated away like cottonwood fluff, I would've gone over the river and away, away into the white meadows beyond the little town of Las Vegas where there was so much early sorrow for me, that I didn't think I'd ever live to see the end of it.

Left to right, this is a photo of my two brothers. Jessy, Me wearing
white shoes, and Ereasmo holding his dog.

Not Much To Do Nights

Growing up at 1801 Montezuma Street was either very dull or very danger-ous, depending on where you were and especially at night. But it wasn't danger-ous outside. Only inside. Still, you never knew when a storm would come up from any direction inside the house. No outer weather was ever as wicked as the inner weather I experienced when I was growing up – or trying to, I might add.

As for amusements, we didn't have any – just the ones we invented. No TV until I was thirteen. We did have a small radio in the kitchen but we weren't sup-posed to listen to it if Wille was sleeping, and he was often sleeping. He slept on the living room sofa, two rooms away from the kitchen, and somehow, even asleep, he managed to hear what we were saying to each other.

Well, we worked our way around that. We whispered, used sign language, and we also used Pig Latin. That way we could communicate with each other and Wille had no idea what we were saying. If we had someone to meet, or if we were going out somewhere, Wille couldn't find out our plans because it was all said in Pig Latin.

Mom, on the other hand, could understand it and even speak it whenever she wanted to keep Wille in the dark. He didn't like this and he'd say – *Que tanto platican? Que es lo que dicen?* What's all this talking, what are these kids saying?

The kitchen was our meeting place for just about everything. Once in a blue moon, we'd have a family meal in the dining room, but that was usually on Sunday when Wille's mom, Grandma Teresa came over for a sit down meal after church. Mama would fix fried chicken, mashed potatoes, brown gravy, tortillas or home baked bread, and *natillas, a* Spanish pudding. We also enjoyed a family meal for some holidays.

Visits from Grandma were nice and it felt good to be together as a family. But I can remember times when father didn't feel like having Grandma over for a visit. He'd watch for her from the living room window as she walked up West National Avenue to our house. He'd lock both the front and the back door and say, "Be quiet!"

We'd hear, *knock-knock* at the front door.

But we weren't allowed to answer.

Moments later, *knock—knock—knock, knock,* at the back door.

Then, finally, silence.

Grandma was gone.

I felt bad for Grandma as I watched her walking down National Avenue and I wondered why her son would treat her like that. But then he treated her no differently than the rest of us.

I was in the fourth grade when one evening while Wille slept on the couch and I sat at the kitchen table. Mom was helping me with my math home work. I was having trouble with math but Mom wouldn't give up on me. She kept explaining the problems, over and over, so it would sink into my little boy brain.

I was complaining when Wille suddenly rushed into the kitchen, half-dressed, grabbed my hair and my neck and slammed my face on the kitchen table. He was yelling at the top of his voice, *Que no entiendes, que no entiendes?* Don't you understand?

Then he stormed back to his place of hibernation.

He left me there, trembling and crying.

My tears dripped on my math book.

After that incident, I always hated math.

And as I got older, I acquired an I-don't-give-a-shit attitude about studying of any kind. This became a problem for the rest of my life as a student. Well, things might change for me, a little here, a little there, but one thing that never changed was Wille's shouting, drinking and physical abuse.

There was the time when Fred literally flew out the back door. I know this story sounds unbelievable, but it really happened.

Fred and I were very young at the time.

Wille came into the kitchen where we were with Mom.

All in one motion, Wille jerked the back door open, kicked the screen door open, grabbed Fred by his heels, twirled him around – and heaved him.

Fred soared out the back door, with the sky overhead and the dusty earth underneath, and when he came in for a landing, he hit his head on a pile of rocks and was knocked out cold.

Mom and I ran out to him. Fred lay perfectly still, sprawled out and seemingly dead. Gently, Mom picked Fred up and brought him into the kitchen. Fred's eyes fluttered open. Mom softly rubbed a cold butter knife on the big lump he had on his head.

I was afraid Fred was going to die.

Miraculously, Fred lived. And amazingly, he didn't have any serious injuries from this. But because of this violent attack, Fred became more distant and there was a growing anger in him towards El Wille.

Another unbelievable thing – the night Wille got drunk and did target practice inside the kitchen.

I don't know where everyone was on this terrible night, but I remember Mom was holding my small brother Ereasmo in her arms as I stood next to her. Ereasmo, at four months, was the baby of the house. I was six and a half at the time.

So there we were standing in the middle of the kitchen floor while madman Wille was shooting in all directions. He shot at the old style clothes washer, the type with the wringer that squeezes water out of the clothes. A bullet hit a steel part of the washer and ricocheted with a whine.

I heard a bullet sing past Mom's face.

We were shaking with fear and Mom and I were praying for Wille to put the gun down and go to sleep. The kitchen smelled of gun smoke, and we were truly afraid for our lives.

I've probably blocked out the rest of it because I don't remember when, or even *if*, he put down the 22. Maybe he kept shooting until he ran out of ammo, I don't know – what I *do* know is that the hand of God was over us that night. Otherwise I don't think I'd be writing this now.

It's so hard to believe that while these horrible things were happening in our house, a Justice of the Peace lived across the street. How could he not know what was going on? He knew, but did nothing, said nothing, and of course, didn't report it. All my life I've wondered about that. The silence and the complicity of certain people who didn't want to get involved.

A Kid Grows Up
Fast On The Streets

Everything starts in the home. That's where I learned to use cuss words; that's where I learned to smoke and drink.

I used to get my father's leftover cigar butts and smoke them. My brother and I knew where he'd hide his wine and whisky bottles too.

Home is also where I learned to harbor anger. Later on, I learned how to express it towards others and the yelling and fighting that I'd learned at home came naturally to me when I took to the streets and stayed out nights getting into trouble.

But basically I was like any other young boy. Hungry for attention, love, affection, respect, appreciation — anything but a fist. Looking for a place of belonging, I was always hungry for a home I didn't have. The streets offered some of what I was searching for, if only on the level of peers respecting you for being tough.

As I've said, even when I was quite young, I was learning to stand up for myself when confronted by bullies. Later on there were gang fights. The streets also introduced me to older guys, more drinking and smoking, and these older guys had cars and liquor too.

So, by the time I was thirteen, I was hanging around with guys in their late teens and early twenties. The one thing I never gave into as a youngster was the use of marijuana or heavy drugs. I wasn't a saint in this, and I did try marijuana a few times when I was in my twenties and thirties. But thanks to God, I never acquired the taste or the need for it. I guess that's one thing I can thank Wille for — he never used drugs, as far as I knew, just booze. Though that is a drug in itself.

Hanging with the older boys exposed me to all the activities that older guys did. Most of them had cars, which gave them the opportunity to pick up girls. A young boy in a car with older girls — that *was* exciting, and very tempting.

45

There was always some girl (or girls) who liked making out with a younger kid. Sex, well, that came easy too. The streets were changing me and as time went on I grew more defiant towards my father and my home life. I was also taking more and more chances . . .

One night, I was in a car accident where I could have easily lost my life. Three of us were in a car following another car full of guys that were partying with us. We were traveling fast on New Mexico Avenue. Our driver was trying to catch up to the guys in the other car, but they were way ahead of us, so he did a hard hairpin turn onto Hot Springs Boulevard heading south to make up some extra time.

Traveling sixty miles an hour in a twenty five mile per hour zone, we caught up quickly to the other car. In fact, our driver slammed the brakes so we wouldn't rear-end the guy ahead of us.

As a result, our car rolled twice, tore down a full length of a fence on the eastside of Hot Springs Boulevard, bounced to the right and landed back on its wheels while crashing into the solid rock wall of what is known as *Arroyo Manteca*. In the car were, the driver, my friend Johnny, sitting in the middle, and me sitting on the passenger's side, with a bottle of wine stuck between my legs.

I braced myself a second before the impact and when we hit the wall, I saw the windshield shatter in front of my eyes. Glass flew like crystal shrapnel, a million tiny pieces of razor sharp glass.

The car bounced back a few feet and the engine died. The three of us got out of the car, shook the glass off our clothing, and stood there for a while in total shock, amazed that none of us were hurt. The neighbors' house lights went on, then we heard sirens, and we knew the police were on their way. The driver told Johnny and me to run. "Get the hell out of here and don't tell nobody you were with me!"

My friend and I ran down the Arroyo de Manteca headed east towards North Gonzales Street. Then we walked to Johnny's house. I knew the protective force was with me that night but on occasions like this, when I was acting so crazy, I wondered why.

There was another time when my friends and I were swimming in Storrie Lake. I didn't know how to swim, nor did I ever learn. That day, all my friends were jumping and diving off the wooden ramp that was located on the west side of the lake. There I was, playing the macho guy dressed in my swim trunks, but scared shitless to get in the water. After standing there seeing all the fun my friends were having – they were diving and swimming all around – I followed my own crazy impulse and ran and jumped into the lake.

Of course I sank like a stone. I was taking in water while pawing my way to the surface while I tried to grab onto someone. Then I sank again and took in more water and I surely would've drowned but for my longtime friend, Ray Herrera, El Cowboy, as we called him. Ray saw that I was in real trouble and not just fooling around. He jumped in and hauled me out. Good old Ray saved my life. His father was called *El Vaquero*, so we called Ray, El Cowboy, but now, in my mind, and ever after, he was also Aquaman.

When I was in the sixth and also seventh grade, I used to work for my cousin, Pita, who was married to Alfredo Ciddio. They owned a liquor store and a small café on Bridge Street. Ray's father owned *El Vaquero* bar, also on Bridge Street and sometimes would leave Ray alone to run the liquor store for short periods at a time. Ray would call me at the restaurant, place an order which included a full chicken, potato along with all the trimmings. When ready, I would walk up the street to El Vaquero's Bar, to deliver Ray's order. While, there, Ray and I would go into the back gambling room. Ray would bring out a quart of ice cold beer, Bud or Coors. We sat at a gambling table and shared the quart while Ray ate his chicken. When finished, I would collect the money for the order, walk back to the restaurant and continue working. So you can readily see that while growing up, I always found myself in situations that involved liquor. Well, why not? I grew up around it.

Risky Telling My Story

My sisters may say, even today, after all these years – " No—You don't want to write about those things. Us running out of the house out onto the streets!"

I don't blame some of my sisters for saying this or for feeling this way. After all, it's risky sharing one's past. Some of us want it to be kept quiet. Other don't mind telling – but to whom?

I'm sure my sisters have some very dark memories, horrific ones, I'm sure, but you don't hear about them too often.

As best I can remember, I was about nine years old when the following story happened. Wille was very drunk and his yelling and cursing had driven Mom and several of us kids out into the dark cool March night.

I was standing out in the front yard alongside my mother, my eldest sister, Juliette, the younger sisters, Theresa and Elizabeth, and little Ereasmo, who was barely three years old. I don't remember where Fred was that night.

I do remember I was holding Ereasmo's hand with my sisters standing just in back of us.

Wille stood on the front porch, face red with rage. He was cursing so loud the whole neighborhood could hear it. *Y tu,-cabroncito!* He was pointing at me and saying, *No me vuelvas a llamar los chotas, te voy a matar.* And you, bastard, don't you ever call the police on me or I will kill you! Wille glared at me. In his threatening right hand was an eight inch kitchen knife. He was mad because I *had* called the police on him.

Under the light of the moon, we could see the bright spit shooting out of his mouth while his hollering brought on a coughing fit that was sprinkled with more curses and threats.

With every wave of his arm, the knife sliced through the cold air. He took another step closer to us and we all slowly took another step backward, our eyes trained on El Wille.

When he was about ten feet away, Wille lunged toward us and we yelled and ran out the front gate. (Yes, the same gate he had destroyed). I stayed with

Mom. I was also dragging little Ereasmo by the hand. The sisters by this time had vanished into the night.

Our screaming could be heard by all of our neighbors as we ran for our lives, with El Wille closing in and swiping the long knife as he continued his wild oaths.

We headed north up Montezuma street towards the corner of Valencia. Every neighbor turned on their front porch light to see what the noise was all about. This distraction caused El Wille to slow down. He stopped in the middle of the street. He was still making noise and brandishing the big knife.

We were under the street light on the corner of Montezuma and Valencia. My hand still clenched Ereasmo's.

Then, one by one, the sisters started to appear. One from behind a light pole, the other two from behind a pile of rocks.

El Wille, screaming with his long knife stumbled back home.

Back, no doubt, to fetch his bottle.

We watched him walking, wavering, his shadow moving jagged under the streetlight.

We didn't know what to do or where to go, so we walked to Grandpa's house. This was Mom's dad who lived about four miles away. Grandpa rented a very small apartment behind his landlord's home on north Gonzales near the corner of Taos Street. It must have been surprising for my poor old grandfather to suddenly have his only daughter and her five children show up this way, all frightened and crazed in his tiny apartment.

That night we slept wherever we could find a place to crash. I don't recall how long we stayed at Grandpa's, a few days, maybe more. Then early one evening as I was playing outside, I heard one of my sisters call my name. "Joseph, be quiet. Dad's outside on the front porch talking to the landlord. Get in here now."

Soon El Wille would be at the door.

What could we do? We couldn't stay at Grandpa's house forever, we knew that, so, in the end, with nowhere else to go, we piled into Wille's car, knowing he was going to take us back home.

Not a whisper was heard from any of us, including Mom. We were all thinking about what was going to happen when Wille got us back home. All the while, I wondered if he planned to fulfill his threat to kill me with that long knife.

When we got home, we marched into the house like silent prisoners.

Strangely, Wille was also quiet. Maybe hung over. Certainly not contrite, for that wasn't his nature.

The hard part, for me, for any of us, was the cold fact that not a single neighbor called the police when they heard us screaming that night. We were running from a wild El Wille with his big knife, and no one had come to help. No one had called for help. No one had done anything but peek and peer from behind drawn curtains.

Of course, as a kid, I reasoned things out a little differently than I do now. I figured it this way — *They didn't call the police because they didn't have telephones.*

It didn't occur to me that they didn't want to get stabbed.

Nor that the entire block of old adobe and brick and wooden houses was part of an ancient, almost tribal landscape where for hundreds of years people didn't tell on people, people didn't speak their mind unless called on to do so by some authority.

It did occur to me that there was no authority greater than the *patron* of our family, the father, El Wille, El Jeffe, the boss.

And this was the way it was in other homes too.

Bully Boys

The year was 1963 and I was in the ninth grade at West Las Vegas Junior High School. That is always such a tough year for students, the transition into high school. Classes are tougher and in the sixties there was a lot of bullying. In my memory, there were two types of male students – those who bullied and those who were bullied. It was macho tough guys, the *pachucos*, who preyed upon the weaker, smaller guys, of which I was one. I was fair game for anyone who wanted to beat me up.

There was a kid named Albert, who liked taunting and hunting me down. He tried hard to get me to fight him. One thing about Albert, he never traveled alone, and I mean, never. He always had a gang of other bullies with him and they foamed at the mouth to get me to fight back. Once in a while, I used to carry a knife for protection but I never pulled it out on Albert.

One night there was a dance at the Historic Plaza Hotel. In those days, the dance hall was in the Northwest end of the building. I was sitting on a window ledge just listening to the music and watching the dancers.

Suddenly, Albert came up beside me. A quick slash of his right hand and I felt warm blood running down my cheek. I stayed where I was, wondering what to do. In Albert's hand I saw a can opener sharpened to a knife edge. He'd slashed me, and I was wet with my own blood, as I sat there in total confusion, Albert walked off with a laugh. But from that night on, I vowed to buy a gun and carry it with me, and the next time Albert attacked me, I'd surprise him.

There is more to it than that – I had a girlfriend to protect, so it wasn't just about me. It was about the two of us, and the one of him and all of them. Albert and his gang of petty henchmen were going to learn a lesson once and for all. So I thought.

But I never did buy a gun, and now I am so glad I didn't.

I was small for my age and weighed 120 pounds. Being light and fast enabled me to beat the guys at track, but as yet it hadn't helped me at close quarters. I knew how to fight – at least I thought I did. But any kid who takes beatings at home doesn't want more of the same at school. I tended to shy away from violence, especially when it stalked me.

Basketball in the school gym was another rough time in my life because there was another bully there named Joe. This guy loved to test me out on the court. He'd mouth-off with all kinds of nasty, sexist jokes about my girlfriend. He talked loud enough for the other team members to hear him.

Joe was short-not quite five feet tall, but he was very husky and strong, and mean. Albert was like him, both excellent athletes in football and basketball, but hard-hearted and violent.

Looking back, I think they could have gone on to play college sports and maybe even professional sports if only they'd honored their God-given talent for athletics, but sadly, they, like a lot of us, had no support at home. No one standing with them and praising them except "the gang." At least, this was my opinion of them.

Day or night, I never knew what kind of mood I was going to be in. It might be dark outside and I'd feel all lit up inside with love for my girlfriend. Or it might be bright and beautiful, but because of the things I've mentioned and my father's temper at home, I'd slip into a depression of desolation and fear. Whatever happened that day, or that night, made me the way I was – a pressure-cooker of unresolved feelings.

I was a member of the West Las Vegas "Gents" basketball team and even though I always showed up for practice, the coach would rarely play me. I guess I wasn't good enough. Eventually I discovered my own temper. Once I was "pissing mad" there was no holding me back. I didn't care who it was, how big or how strong the guy was, or how many guys were attacking me, I got scrappy and fought back. Usually, because I was small, I got my ass kicked, but I didn't care because at least I stood up for myself.

One day during basketball practice, Joe was harassing, as usual. All through practice he kept making ugly sexual comments about my girlfriend. This went on all during practice, Joe's dirty remarks, the other players laughing. ("Yah, I laid her on a desk, and she liked it.")

He went on this way and when practice was over, I was insanely mad. But he didn't stop there. He continued his jibes inside the locker room. I just kept taking his shit while we were in the shower, but I could feel the pressure rising in me and I didn't know how long I could keep myself under control. Finally, when I was fully dressed, combing my hair at the mirror, Joe stood right next to me, and made some more rotten remarks.

I'd had all I could take — suddenly I blew up — and out poured a flood of cuss words, screams, threats, and challenges. I told him, "Okay, let's see how tough you are." In New Mexico Spanglish it sounds much more threatening — "Vamos of ver que tal jodon estas." This was real *in your face type of shit!*

Joe came at me like a bull with every animal muscle in his body ready to stomp me. It's kind of funny that as I am writing about this now, I get a vivid picture in my mind of the dressing room where the fight took place. All the basketball team members gathered around the room, packed in like spectators at a boxing match. Many are standing on the benches howling, laughing, hollering nasty words in Spanish like: *dale jodasos, chingalo.*

I didn't know if they are cheering for me or Joe, but I felt the anger bursting out of me with every punch or kick I threw. All the anger I'd harbored for so long came out like a rip tide of fury. I was fighting — not one guy but all the bullies in the school.

But it was much more than that as I've said earlier — deep down, I'm venting many years of stored-up anger towards my father, the biggest bully in my life, and I have to land some really hard punches to stop him from beating me and my mother. So it's Joe and not El Wille, but it doesn't matter to me who it is.

There I am dancing all around the shower and dressing room, sometimes he throws me on top of a bench and pounds me all over the head and body. But each time, I'm able to fight him off. Then he comes back harder and I'm pinned in a corner on the floor. Joe's like a small bull, solid and strong, and me, well, I'm the bantam rooster, flying in and around so swiftly he can't really hurt me, and meanwhile I'm throwing blows of my own and they're connecting more often than not.

Coach Frank Herrera hears us battling and he comes into the locker room, and sees Joe and me in a clinch and, to my surprise, coach Herrera doesn't stop the fight. He just stands guard at the door and lets us go at each other.

Finally, I'm worn out, finished.

So's Joe.

We stop fighting.

Amidst the cheers, the jeers and the yells, we both get up and go to the big mirrors, wash the blood off our faces with cold water, comb our hair with shaky hands, straighten out our clothing, and all the while we're breathing heavily and the adrenalin is rushing through us.

But I feel really good inside, because even though I took a lot of licks, even though I might've got my ass kicked, it doesn't matter at all to me. What matters is this — I fought back.

I'm hurting all over on the outside, but on the inside, I know I won the battle. Not against Joe. But against all the odds against me, including the fear of fighting itself.

I've won on the inside, and no one can take that away now.

Not even my father.

I Have Not Yet Begun To Fight

As it turned out, there were many more fights that came my way. That did not surprise me. I didn't know if it was because a lot of guys didn't seem to like me, or maybe I somehow pissed them off and turned them against me.

One thing that might've made them mad at me was that the girl I was dating was really cute and the other guys who were also after her probably wondered why she'd chosen the little skinny guy.

Now there were these twins, brothers, at our school, Richard and Roger and they were one grade ahead of me. One of the brothers was after my girl. One night after basketball practice, the twins and another friend of theirs named Jessie Ortega, decided to beat me up.

I didn't know they had talked Jessie into doing their bidding for them. Their plan was to get me to fight Jessie, and then, at the right moment, they'd jump in too.

The fight was to take place in front of the junior high building. This was a beautiful old wooden school that burned down sometime in the 1970s.

The deal was that we'd carry on until we mutually agreed to stop fighting or were just too tired to continue. I handed my duffle bag and tennis shoes, which were hanging over my right shoulder, to one of my friends. The minute Jessie and I started walking towards the front of the school, the twins slipped around the back of the building to wait for the right moment to pounce. But they didn't get very far. My friend, Victor, quickly saw their plan. He grabbed the twins by the neck and told them, "If you try to jump Joseph, I'm going to kick your ass myself." That shut them down. Victor was one tough guy and they didn't want any trouble from him.

Anyway, they joined the crowd that had gathered to see the fight.

Jessie, just like Albert and Joe, was a football and basketball player, and he also lifted weights. But what made this fight different was that we both agreed to shake hands afterward. That at least gave it some degree of dignity as far as I was concerned. Who knows — win or lose — we might end up friends.

So Jessie and I shook hands and he let the first blow fly and, yes, he connected with his blow. My advantage, if I had one, was that I was lightweight and could move swiftly. I wasn't carrying a lot of weight, like he was, and I was fast as a ferret.

So there we were fighting under the stars and a bright moon.

Jessie came at me real quick and I backed up and tripped on the edge of the sidewalk and fell onto the concrete, landing on my back. Jessie jumped on top of me, straddling my body. Then he grabbed me by the hair and started banging my head on the sidewalk. This he repeated, again and again. With every bang, the night all around my eyes and inside my head lit up like a Roman candle. I saw flashing lights and then I felt faint, and I don't have to say that I was in desperate trouble but even so — dizzy and in pain — I worked my right leg high in the air and curled it around Jessie's neck. This gave me a sudden advantage and I somehow managed to flip him off me. Looking back, it's hard for me to believe I was able to do this to a strong weightlifter type guy like Jessie.

We went at it like this for about a half hour.

Then we both ended the fight, shook hands and walked back to where the crowd was waiting. Everyone must have thought it strange as we arrived because on the way we were laughing and joking about the fight. It was, in fact, just as I imagined it might be, and once again, I felt fulfilled inside. Not so much because I'd defended myself and got in a few good punches and kicks, but because I knew I'd made a new friend.

We certainly *did* become good friends. Jessie would invite me to his home after school so we could lift weights together. After that, he'd invite me to join him at the table and share a meal prepared by his mother.

At school we hung out together. I think this served to send a positive message to other students at school because everyone knew about our fight and they saw we were now close friends.

Albert, on the other hand, didn't like the idea. Remember Albert? The other bully that was always trying to beat me up. Jessie once in a while hung around with him and both came from the same neighborhood, so I think Albert sort of felt betrayed by Jessie because he was hanging around with me, and this weakened Albert's macho image with his friends. In fact, Jessie and I became such good friends, that Jessie would even stand up for me whenever Albert wanted to bang on me.

One night during a West Las Vegas Dons football game, Albert and his gang of twelve tried to force me to get into a fight in the boys bathroom. This time my anger at them didn't get me into trouble. Albert had been after me for the past two years and would have loved nothing more than to leave me bloody and beaten in that bathroom.

I looked into Albert's eyes, saw they were glassy, watery, red with rage. He had one of those permanent smirks on his lips. Well, rumor had it he was a druggy, and this night he looked that way.

Perkins Stadium, where the game was being played, was jam packed and by now a crowd was all around Albert and me.

I glanced up and saw Jessie, he was standing towards the back of the crowd, and he gave me a signal with his eyes and a shake of the head not to go down into the bathroom and fight Albert. I realized he was there for support and he kept signaling me with his eyes, saying, "Don't fight Albert."

Then, for some reason, the crowd broke up, dispersed. Albert blew off some steam, swore at me, and then he and his followers took off, and that was the end of it.

* * *

Today, I still don't know what happened to Albert in later life. He may have passed away. Joe's still around Las Vegas and I see him from time to time. And my old guardian-friend, Jessie? Well, I don't know what happened to him either. Sometimes I find myself thinking about him, wishing I could see him and give him a hug and shake his hand. But all during this turmoil time of my life, the terrible fights I had to endure, and the humiliations from my father, I always felt the strong, indefinable, at that time, powerful presence around me. Maybe I questioned it back then, maybe I didn't. But now I know that it was the protective presence that was with me from childhood, and when a friend like Jessie came along and stood up for me, well I can look back now and know that he, too, was a messenger of faith.

A Cold Night In Hell

I have mentioned that my brother Fred and I were the only boys at home for a number of years. This was until our younger brother Ereasmo came along. Fred and I shared many of the same experiences and our memories often intertwine. In some cases, I might have been too young to remember things as vividly as Fred and he has given me fresh accounts of things that happened to him. The other day he wrote this memoir of his own and I repeat it here in Fred's own voice and just as he wrote it;

Familia Abandonada, una noche fria y Nevada
Abandoned Family, on a cold snowy night

I remember it was snowing and it must have been one of the coldest nights in Las Vegas back then. The story starts with "El Willé Moto" as I used to call my father. He wanted to take all of us out for a ride in the faded green jalopy he parked in the back yard. Not the Chief Pontiac with the glowing hood ornament. That car came later.

I remember it was starting to get dark, when all of us got into the *chalupa*, as we called it then. I don't really remember the route he took but I do remember him sliding on the icy roads as if it was a big joy ride – to him. It was me, Liz, Juliette, Theresa and I'm not sure if Jeannette was there…but it must have been you, Joseph, in Mama's arms because the younger ones weren't born yet.

After what seemed like a very long ride, *El Wille Moto*, which was only a nickname I'd given him, decided to stop at a bar he frequented to buy a bottle of wine. *"Dejame ir a comprar un vinito"*. Let me go and buy a little bottle of wine. I remember him telling Mama. I think the bar was called La Cantina on south Grand and Lincoln Avenue across from Lions Park.

I don't remember where he parked but I do remember him getting out of the car and walking to La Cantina in the deep drifts of snow.

"He didn't come back.

I remember that all of us waited in the chalupa for a very long time. We were young, cold, and miserable. The chalupa was like an empty van with no seats in the back, and the metal was cold to the touch and it burned when we drew the air into our lungs. After more than an hour, Mama made the decision to start walking home with all of us.

It was around nine at night. Mama carried Joseph and sometimes two or three more children as well. She trudged along through the windy snowy night. The wind made it hard to breathe.

We lived at 1801 Montezuma Street and West National Avenue. From La Cantina to our house, it's a good two and a half mile walk.

As the eldest son, I walked the whole time. It was very difficult with the snow up to my waist and falling into my shoes. But poor Mama never had good shoes and her feet *had* to be colder than mine, and she simply trudged along uncomplaining.

None of us had shoes for this kind of weather.

I kept asking her, "Are we almost there?"

"Just keep walking," Mama repeated.

So we did.

I don't remember what time it was when we returned home…but I do remember how cold I was when we got there.

* * *

Fred's memory of that bad night reminds me now that our father had no concept of what his actions might have done to his wife and his children. Did he know that he put us in danger? Of course not. Had he known, he wouldn't have done it. El Wille had but one thing on his mind — a bottle of wine.

Again, I realize how blessed we were to have a strong, compassionate mother. My family and I are doubly blessed to have survived such painful experiences, and to have come out of them without contempt for the man who perpetrated these things so unknowingly.

Sometimes I wonder — did he ever know?

In writing of my past and the hurtful things my father did to my mother, my brothers and sisters and me, I don't mean to be disrespectful or belittle my father's memory. I write because I know there is liberation in not allowing unresolved memories to haunt me. For, if they linger in that way, they'll surely poison my mind and spirit.

So this book is not about hate, regrets or revenge towards my father. This isn't about my father, really, it's about accepting and understanding my past. It's about reaching out to the lost boy who had so much promise and love in him. In finding that little boy, I rejoice in finding myself as an adult. This is why I'm writing my story.

I thank God for these difficult, and sometimes, nearly impossible, childhood experiences.

For without them, I wouldn't be who I am today. I wouldn't have discovered my true self – a man with a willing heart and an open mind, a man who was once a sad and embittered boy wondering why his father treated him so badly. A father who sometimes wanted to get rid of his family and probably himself.

Sometimes the facts of life speak for themselves. Without my father, I would not have been born and there would be no story to tell, no book to write. So, even if some of these experiences appear to be negative and destructive – and as a child I perceived them as such – in reality, they are the tools I was given, the learning tools that saved my life rather than ended it.

Jailbird

Most of the time when I was a teenager, I was searching for love.

Young, troubled and unhappy, I looked to the opposite sex for love, help, justification, companionship. It's a little hard for me to believe that I found these things in one girl when I was in the fifth grade.

How silly of me. What did I know about love at so young an age? As I got older, I became increasingly possessive, sometimes dangerously so. No boy could even look at my girl without my permission. I was insanely protective, and this didn't help things with her because she already had problems at home – a crazy father like mine.

By eleventh grade, Mary Lou, or Mitzi as everyone called her, was tired of my fanatical and possessive ways, but when we first met and for many years after, there were good times and bad, but mostly good.

The way we met, Mitzi and her father came into the restaurant where I worked for my cousin Pita and her husband Alfredo Ciddio. Mitzie's father, Benny and Alfredo were brothers. I was immediately attracted to her pretty smile and glowing eyes and soon we started seeing each other without her parent's knowledge.

When things started to cool between us, it was because Mitzi started seeing another boy and I'd gotten so jealous that I almost killed him. Here is exactly how that happened.

Her parents would go out dancing or maybe to the movies. One night, she, her uncle Manual, (who was also her age), and a couple of other boys, including the guy she was with, had gone out together. I had gone to her house looking for her and found out she was with them. So I waited for her in the family's open garage doorway. After a few hours, the headlights of their car lit up the dark night and they saw me standing there and my anger took over.

I grabbed a large rock to smash the car windshield. *No, that would hurt the other innocent people in the car.* I dropped the rock, walked up to the passenger back door just as it opened and the boy, Bobby Martinez, slid out of the car.

Out of my jacket pocket came my gravity knife. I flicked the blade open, grabbed Bobby by the shoulder with my left hand and pulled him towards me. Full force, I plunged the knife into his stomach.

Bobby doubled over, dropped to his knees.

A wild scream rang out from one of the other boys – *"He stabbed him, he stabbed him!"* – I stood there as if time had frozen. The seriousness of what I'd had done wasn't clear to me yet, but I felt cold, dead and unable to move.

"You have to go with them to the hospital," Mitzi cried out. She begged me right there in the darkness while he was bleeding in the dirt.

"Hell no," I said, "Let the son of a bitch die."

My voice didn't sound like me.

They rushed Bobby to the hospital and I stood there watching the car's tail lights burn into the black night and disappear.

Then, I realized what I'd done. I am so sorry Bobby.

I ran home, came inside, said nothing to my mom.

Willé wasn't there – good thing.

After a little while, there came a knock at the kitchen door. I knew exactly who it was as I was hiding behind the wood stove listening. The police officer asked my frightened mother where I was and before she could answer he told her what had happened.

I stood behind the stove remembering how an innocent little boy named Joseph used to stand in that same place and throw cold water on my sisters when they were taking their bath in the old *cajete.*

The difference was, this Joseph was an older, colder, spiteful kid. From behind the stove, head bowed down, I came into the kitchen. I could see the officer at the back door. Time moved strangely – neither fast nor slow. I seemed to be watching myself, as if in a movie. I looked at my mother's face, saw her fearful eyes with the tears rolling down. The officer put handcuffs on me, walked me to the squad car. The door was open, waiting for me.

Moments later, he drove away with me in the back seat still looking at my mother bathed in the yellow light coming from the open kitchen doorway, as she stood pitifully in the sad night watching her little Joseph being taken away to the San Miguel County Jail.

Later I was sitting with another kid, a jailbird who was shooting out thousands of questions, wanting to know what I'd done. Why was I there? What had happened? How did I do it?

I didn't feel like talking.

By now, I too had a thousand questions of my own. *Why did I stab Bobby? What's going to happen to me? Is Bobby going to die?* The jailer emptied everything out of my pockets while processing my jail file.

I had a piece of steel wool and a copper ring I was making in school. These alone had stayed stuck in my pocket. That helped me pass the time away as I sat on my bunk polishing the ring and staring out the barred window, longing to be with my mom just up one block from the court house, so close and yet so far. At that moment I felt separated from everything I knew and had once loved. Myself included.

In the afternoons, when school was out, I'd watch the students as they passed the court house. Some times I would call out and whistle to the pretty girls as they walked by. Some of my friends would stand out- side and shout my name so that I would come to the window. *Ese vato. Joseph, como te va?* Hey Joseph, how's it going?

"Bring me some cigarettes" I'd say.

To tell the truth, I can't remember how long I was in jail.

But it seemed like lonely long days and endless nights.

As it turned out, Bobby and his family refused to file charges, so, after a while I was released under probation. My conditions of release were that I had to see a probation officer each week as I've mentioned in an earlier story. This I've also shared, that while growing up, there were many times when I felt a comforting presence around me.

The day I was released from jail, it all happened so quickly and it seemed very strange to me how it all came about. I was in my jail cell, the jailer came to my cell door, opened it, told me I was free to go. He handed over my belongings and sent me on my way. I didn't want to go home because I knew what was waiting for me.

Another fight.

A horrible beating from El Wille.

I had nowhere to go — but home.

But I was in no hurry to get there.

Slowly, I walked down the two flights of stairs, out to the main hallway and headed straight to the front door exit facing West National Avenue that led straight to my house only one block away. I felt very weird about walking into my house because once I was in, I knew I'd have to run out again – with El Wille on my tail!

I opened the front door of the court house and walked outside into the sunlight.

Then, clear as a bell, I heard a voice.

Actually, more like a strong thought telling me, *Go out the back door.*

Now, why, after already taking the front exit, would I stop, turn around, go back inside, walk down the long hallway to go out the back way?

It made no sense but I followed the voice and reversed my direction.

Remember, though, I already felt pretty strange.

The way I was released – no one explained anything to me, the officer just said I was free to go.

The awkwardness of returning home . . . the fear of reprisals from Wille or the gang that protected Bobby. . . these things were rattling around in my head.

Well, I reached the back exit, opened the door, and as I looked out at the parking lot I saw someone.

The man was leaning against his car, arms crossed. It was Servando Lucero, my brother-in-law (married to my sister Jeannette, the eldest of the sisters) and so I called out to him, "What are you doing here, Servando?

"Didn't they tell you I got you out of jail, and that I'd be waiting for you out here?"

"No one told me anything," I replied.

I knew, once again, that I was in the presence of that friendly force that I'd experienced so many times in the past. Why did I ever question it?

I learned from Servando that I was going to stay with Jeannette and him. My brother Fred was going to continue picking me up in the morning and driving me to school and he'd take me home at noon for lunch, then back to Servando's in the afternoon.

Jeannette and Servando owned a small neighborhood store on Independence Street where they lived. They also owned some apartments on the same property. That would be my place of work after school every day and weekends. Servando assigned many duties to me, which included sanding and painting the apartments, fixing floors, and also pulling weeds and raking up trash around the yard. In those old apartments, the ancient water lines were always busting or freezing during the winter. So my job also included performing something for which I had plenty of former experience – ditch digging.

But I also got good at fixing ruptured pipes.

Inside the building I made myself useful by helping my sister clean house and baby sitting my nephews, Ivan and Phillip who were still small babies. I learned how to bathe them, change dirty diapers, and how to prepare their formulas and put them to bed. I used to do this when Jeannette and Servando went out to the movies or out to eat in a local restaurant.

Life wasn't all that bad any more. For one thing, I wasn't wasting away in the county jail. But I still had problems – for one thing, my probation officer wouldn't allow me to attend any school functions like games or night dances, and for another, my heart was sad because I wasn't permitted to see my girlfriend.

In time, the restrictions and the constant work got to me. Even though I wasn't under threat of El Willé, I still got depressed sometimes and I became very introverted. While working in the apartments, I used to smoke quite often. I was allowed some times to enjoy a cold beer while painting the rooms, and that was nice.

But overall I began to feel discouraged about life – by its sameness and its iron-clad rules. I adopted an indifferent attitude about things. Gradually, as time went on, I stopped caring about myself or my future.

I cried a lot because I was lonely; I missed not seeing my mother.

The inner voice that had set me free wasn't available to me at that time – or so I believed. I waited for it. But it didn't come. Maybe I couldn't hear it any more, I don't know.

One day, falling into a deep depression as I was working in the apartments, I impulsively decided to end it all. I turned on the gas valve of a wall heater, let the gas escape into the apartment I was painting, and then I sat down beside the heater, lit a cigarette, and waited for the gas to ignite and blow up.

After a few minutes though I came to my senses and switched off the gas valve.

That was when I learned that, sometimes, the voice wasn't a voice at all. It was a feeling that simply commanded me to do the right thing.

I believe I stayed with my sister and her husband for over a year, then I was allowed to go back home. I don't know if that was a good thing for me or not, because now I was back in the home that had always been such a bad place for me, and I never knew what to expect from El Wille.

Nor would I.

Family Matters

My cousin Pita and her husband, Alfredo inherited the liquor store that my aunt Martina used to own, along with a leather and boot shop right next door. Tia Martina did not have the restaurant, only the liquor store and leather shop. My father used to visit her nights and take me and my sister Theresa along. While they drank till all hours of the night, Theresa and I would sit at the antique player piano my aunt owned and we would play it all night long.

Later, when I was a little older but not much, I would work for my Tia Martina cleaning, empting trash and sweeping her shop. After my Tia Martina passed away, Pita and Alfredo kept the liquor store operating and soon opened up a small café where I would eventually work. I was trained to do everything – cooking, taking orders, waiting tables and of course, bussing and cleaning tables. I was the dishwasher too, and I learned how to manage the cash register. At closing time, which was at nine o'clock at night, I cleaned the restaurant, swept the floors, and did food prep for the following day. I also washed the front windows and swept the sidewalk.

Other duties included emptying the trash cans several times a day, for both the restaurant and the liquor store. Alfredo and Pita were in the restaurant during the day but they had a buzzer that told them if someone had entered the liquor store where customers were less frequent during the daylight hours.

When I was in the liquor store picking up the trash, I'd open the sliding doors to the refrigerator where the ice cold beer was kept. I'd grab a quart of beer, put it into the trash can, lay a newspaper, the Daily Optic, over it, then walk outside to the back of the building. While unloading the trash I'd take a swallow from that cold quart of beer. No wonder I liked taking out the trash – no one could keep me from it!

Let me also say that there were some fun family times that I remember. Maybe they were few and far between but there were times when El Wille was actually Dad. There were times when he would drive us to Mora, New Mexico where Uncle Pete lived. He was my father's brother. He owned a mechanic garage and small restaurant. My mother was born in Guadalupita, New Mexico, and at summer time we often visited our uncle Abel, who was my mother's father's only brother.

I loved visiting Tio Abél, seeing him and being with him was like going back in time. His house was a long and high adobe home with no indoor plumbing or electricity. He used old oil lamps and the floors were all dirt. The house had a musty smell to it, but it was cool in the summer, and warm in the winter. He owned a lot of property which fronted the Mora River and he had large apple orchards. Fred and I used to help him haul water from the river and his well. I miss those days.

When we drove there, we always found him on horseback moving his cattle from one pasture to another. He was very tall, thin and dark skinned. He had the strong features of an American Indian and spoke only Spanish. When Uncle Abél and Grandpa died, my mother and her brother, my uncle Joe, inherited about 160 acres of land. Some in my family think it was about 400 to 600 acres of land. I really am not sure. All I know is that the land my mother inherited, she sold, or actually gave away for a small amount of money. Why? Again because stubborn Wille had no interest, vision or initiative to take the land and do something productive with it. Maybe he just wanted the easy money.

Other good times were when our father would drive us north of town past the Silver Spur eatery to watch movies at the drive-in. We would park out on an empty field where we had a clear view of the big screen. There were two problems with this set up. First, we were too far away to really enjoy the flicks, and we had no sound. But it was free. Visiting the abandoned Old Baca Mansion on Old National Road in Upper Town was a very special treat for me. This mansion was originally owned by one of our family ancestors, Don Jose Albino Baca I.

I remember my father taking mama, my sister Theresa and I to the mansion when it was abandoned. In speaking with Theresa about our visits to the Baca mansion, she believes she was around ten years old. That would have put me at five years of age. I recall going through the entire mansion room by room.

On the second floor, there was an old piano where Theresa and I would bang on the ivory keys and the noise we made echoed throughout the mansion. It was really sad that when the magnificent house was abandoned for many years, local people stole some of the imported wood and other items. They even stole the imported wood trim from the windows, the antique door hinges, and anything that took their fancy.

The history of the mansion and its originator might be summed up as follows . . .

The year was 1851 and the village called Upper Las Vegas is where the *adobes* were laid out for a mansion, a place for the gracious living of a Spanish Don. Not far away was the Santa Fe Trail. Teams of oxen brought lumber for the mansion over the long Trail from what is now Kansas City. The winding stairways were English walnut from St. Louis. The three story mansion contained seventeen rooms, two open patios and many more amenities. The mansion was known for the week long fiestas where governors, political leaders of the day and the rich and powerful businessmen of Las Vegas would come to celebrate, eat, dance and drink and be merry. Many Santa Fe Trail merchants also were frequent visitors to the Baca mansion.

The holidays were rarely observed or celebrated in our Baca home. That also included birthdays. I guess for me, that's why as an adult, my birthday is just another day. Holidays, the same. Our house was probably the only dark house during the Christmas holidays. Maybe we would put up a Christmas tree once in a very long while, but there was no exchanging of presents since there was barely enough money for food and necessities. As I got older, decorating the house didn't mean anything because I was rarely at home. More and more, slowly but surely, home was a place to eat, sleep, wash, study (as little as possible), then hit the streets. The streets were inviting, exciting and they presented a whole new world for me. This kind of haphazard living would last through most of my junior and high school days.

That Old Kitchen Floor

There was nothing to keep me home except Mom and my brothers and sisters. The yelling, drinking, and irrational behavior of El Willé wasn't getting any better — unless you consider *worse* better — so I took to the streets.

Out in the streets with my friends, or making new ones, I could forget all about my problems at home and be myself, or pretend to be whomever I wanted to be.

Out on the streets, I found a way of life that was easy and free and seldom lonely. It was easy to get someone to buy underage kids some liquor, and we could always buy cigarettes, no problem there. Walking the streets and sometimes dodging the bullies took lots of energy, but I always knew I could return home for Mom's delicious meals. It's not like I was homeless, you know. Besides, I was usually welcomed to eat at the home of one of my friends, and thank God for that too.

For me, staying out late was pleasurable and the moment it got dark I somehow felt safer. But this came with the knowledge that I had nowhere else to go — it was either home or the streets. Sometimes though when I wanted to be at home, I found the back door locked and there was no way to get in. I'd knock very quietly a few times. It was more like tapping and hoping that Mom would hear and unlock the door. But that didn't always work. Often she must have heard me tapping, but she was probably frightened that El Wille would hear her letting me in and then of course there'd be hell to pay.

Nights when the kitchen door wasn't locked, I'd come in quiet as a mouse, turning the door knob so that the clicking was so soft it couldn't be heard. All I needed was twelve inches and I could slip in silently. Remember, I was a skinny kid. But it took more quiet time to close the door because it squeaked as most wooden doors do and the hinges complained as well. In the stillness of night, even the slightest movement, seemed loud to me.

Once inside, I was faced with another problem — the obstacle of walking all across the kitchen floor to the bedroom. This seemed more like walking in a mine field, with an explosion awaiting my every step.   But, all us kids had that mastered, too.

When the brothers and sisters were gathered, and El Willé wasn't at home, we shared our tales of coming in late and walking across that creepy kitchen floor. We'd imitate each other's movements with each step on the mine field, moving along undetected until . . .

. . . making a noise like the wooden floorboards, a creaking sound, we'd burst into laughter.

The fact is, when we were doing this for real, there was a real art in the timing and precision and knowing exactly which solid board to plant your foot on. Our after-hours movements had to be synchronized so they were drowned out by El Wille's loud snores. Success could only be achieved by listening . . . you could tell by the depth of the snore how deeply asleep he was. Then, in pitch dark, you had to remember which boards were firm and which were squeaky.

Obviously, this meant memorizing the floor plan.

But hearing the length and breadth of the snore was really critical, and woe to the one who didn't pay attention to it.

If you were in a safe zone and on a good board, you had to hold your position before taking your next step; and this would depend on how long it would be before the next snore.

The obstacle course was only half-finished at the kitchen table. At that point, you were almost there. But next to the table was the wood stove, which most times was still hot from the long day's fire. If you weren't careful there, you'd burn yourself.

This was a little tricky if you'd been drinking beer.

Beyond the stove, a couple more steps, and then, you were in the promised land.

However, the hurdle was to make no noise getting undressed, and then to slip into bed without a sound. Some nights though, when I was drinking, I'd go to bed fully dressed. Better that than getting caught. Even at the end of the obstacle course, El Wille could wake and catch you at the stretch. In which case, you'd get a real licking. Also by staying dressed when you got into bed, you could get out of there in a moment's notice, if need be.

All of us used this same technique. All except Mom. But what I didn't know, until years later talking to my brother Fred, was that he used to imitate me coming in late, so that if El Wille woke and heard *him*, he'd think it was *me*. We laughed and laughed over this funny deception but back in the day, it wouldn't have been funny at all.

Over sixty years later though, if I put my mind to it, I can see the boards that are safe and those that aren't and I can even hear the exact sound the bad boards make, and sometimes, if I'm sound asleep and dreaming, I hear *creeeeek*, and it's me, age fourteen, tiptoeing through my own kitchen nightmare.

A Wild Kid In
The Wild, Wild West

The Montezuma skating ponds were a treasure for our community and the residents of Montezuma, New Mexico. The ponds were made by the Gallinas River which was itself shadowed by a grand and beautiful cliff-face that ran the length of the canyon and village.

The Montezuma Hotel was a place much liked by Theodore Roosevelt and other notables who were there before and after the turn of the 19th century. President Rutherford B. Hayes visited Montezuma and the great boxer Jack Johnson, who also trained at the hotel in the 1920s. Other famous visitors included the notorious outlaw Jesse James.

Few remember today that the Montezuma Hotel was the first building in New Mexico to have electric lighting.

Well, when I was growing up, the castle, as it was called, was filled with black-frocked, Jesuit seminarians from Mexico. They attended school in the old, turreted building in preparation for the priesthood. Some of the monks were expert skaters, as were many locals as well. Skating at the ponds started on Thanksgiving Day and the weekend crowds easily numbered two or three hundred.

This was a family winter wonderland affair with moms and dads and kids skating and having fun. A stone building called the 20/30 club was manned by the local Jaycees. Inside, you could buy soft drinks, hot chocolate, and candy. You could also rent skates. The aroma of hot dogs and burgers frying on grills would fill the small, enchanted valley. Some people lit small fires to keep warm. At night, the glow from the fires illuminated the skating pond and the flames danced twice, once in the nighttime air and again on the ice.

I can still hear the laughter, the squeals, the shrill cries of the skaters as their cries echoed on tall cliffs of Montezuma. I can still see the bundled people, their heavy coats, scarves, caps, gloves. The ladies sliding along like swans, the daredevil boys racing from one end of the pond to the other, while some went at high speed to the water falls, skidding a few feet from the frozen edge in a reckless turn-about of 360 degrees.

I skated all right but mostly my time was spent getting up after landing on my butt. Cars lined up by the ponds and some folks watched from the warmth in their cars, honking whenever their kids skated past. Naturally, the ice ponds were also a trysting place for young lovers and for those who indulged in girl watching, which was my specialty.

The crowds sometimes were so large that cars had to park far away to get there. Many young people who didn't have cars or any way of getting out to the Canyon walked to the ponds from town. But, since many people drove there, walkers usually got rides from friends.

Some of us still remember the wooden canal, or flume, that was attached to the side of the rock cliff fifty or more feet off the ground. In the old days, the canal carried water from up the canyon down to the power plant off the Gallinas River nearby the ponds.

I got to know that canal and so did some of my friends. But it turned out to be a very risky encounter.

One summer's day, a group of us boys (Tony Martinez, his two brothers Carlos and Herman, or Bobby as we called him, and also Fred and I) decided that we were going to walk the flume. This was a distance of about five hundred feet. To get to it, you had to climb the vertical face of the rock cliff.

We started the climb, not giving a second's thought to the possibility that the 85-year-old flume might collapse under our collective weight.

Tony and my brother Fred climbed the cliff very quickly and then the plan was to walk the canal until we reached the waterfall.

So, up the cliff we climbed, carefully seeking safe little crannies for toe-holds. We also sought hand-holds along the cliff-face; I was ahead in the climb, followed by Bob who was right behind me, and then Carlos.

We'd probably climbed about thirty feet up, when a rock tumbled loose under my right foot. It broke off, I started to slide but was able to hang on. I called down — "Watch out, Bobby!" — he looked up just in time to dodge a missile that would've crushed his skull. He ducked and was grazed as the rock plunged past him.

Bobby's screams echoed off the mountainside and could be heard all through the Canyon. He hung on, blood running down his face. The three of us started a quick descent, reaching the ground in a hurry. Then Carlos ran toward the waterfall where Tony and Fred were crossing over.

I stayed with Bobby and tried to stop his bleeding. He was in terrible pain, and the blood kept coming. Once on the ground, Tony ran to a nearby adobe, and called his dad.

It's a fifteen minute drive from Montezuma to Las Vegas. Mr. Martinez got there really fast, then he helped Bobby into the car and got him to the hospital.

As it turned out, the cut was just below Bobby's left eye — no damage to the eye itself, he was going to be okay.

That was the first and last time we ever thought of climbing the cliff to walk on the flume.

But there were other weird misadventures around that same time.

Summer days were often spent walking around town and exploring abandoned buildings, of which there were many in Old Town. One such was the old trolley building near Ninth Street.

Outside was a big, long hose that went twenty feet into the ground. If you pulled on it, a gush of cold water came down on you. This felt refreshing on a hot summer's day, and we took turns (the same group of cliff climbers) taking an icy shower.

The other crazy thing we did was to go underneath Valencia Street right behind the Historic Plaza Hotel. Next to the building was a coal chute. There was a trap door where trucks delivered coal for the Plaza Hotel. That was in the days when they used coal in their boiler to heat the building.

This coal chute also led to the downstairs basement of the building. There was nothing down there but an old pile of musty black coal, a rotten stink, and rats. When we emerged from underground into the bright New Mexico sunlight, we laughed at each other because our skin was jet black from the coal dust.

Across Valencia Street from the Plaza Hotel were the abandoned Ilfeld warehouses. Those buildings weren't locked and we'd walk inside and explore them as much as we wanted. Down Valencia Street on the corner of North Gonzales stood the old San Miguel County Jail where Billy the Kid was once a captive. In our day, the jail was nothing but a shell constructed the old way, out of adobe. One of the windows still had iron bars from the 1800s. Not much for us to do in this small building with its dirt floor and bare walls, but it did offer another place to explore, hang out, and sometimes get a buzz from the historical phantoms that lingered in the legacy of that old place.

The Christian Brother's old school building on the corner of New Mexico Avenue and Valencia Street was another vacant treasure for Fred and me to explore. This building had long outside corridors and many dusty, deserted rooms.

Another memory that won't go away is walking to North Public School where I attended elementary school. One day, I was in charge of taking Ereasmo to school for his registration.

We used to cut across the field where the Christian Brothers building stood. On this day, Ereasmo ran ahead of me. He wouldn't stop even though I hollered at him as loud as I could — "*Stop,* Ereasmo, stop! You're gonna get hit by a car!"

Ereasmo just kept going. He ran down Valencia, across New Mexico Avenue, then back across Valencia toward the empty Christian Brothers lot.

I couldn't believe the little runt could run that fast. So fast I couldn't catch him.

Then, he disappeared.

This was followed by piercing cries of pain.

When I caught up to him, he was lying on the ground and bleeding profusely from under his eye.

I panicked. El Wille's going to really beat me up this time!

What had happened was Ereasmo had run into a strand of barbed-wire that was strung across the property. I didn't know what to do, so I rushed him home, half-pulling, half-dragging him. Ereasmo screamed the entire way. I hated him for doing this and, selfishly, I was more concerned about what was going to happen to *me* than I was about what had just happened to *him.*

Fortunately, Mama cleaned him up before El Wille got home. I can't remember if we went back to school that day. But I do remember that he didn't hurt his eye.

I don't recall if El Wille ever found out about this little caper of Ereasmo's. Memory says no.

But even now I get a little chill, thinking of it.

Because the punishment didn't fit the crime.

Unless it's a crime to be a kid.

The Accident That
Saved My Life

The summer of 1957 when I was eleven years old, my brother Fred and I hung around with the Martinez brothers. We used the pond on the Gallinas River northeast of the old State Hospital. We'd go there on summer days to swim, fish and mess around.

We didn't have fishing rods, the kind you buy in a store. We had a branch off a tree, some nylon line and a hook. One day fishing at the pond off the Gillinas, I was standing behind Fred when he swung back to cast his line. No one saw it happening but me.

When Fred jerked his line forward, it caught on something.

There were screams – this time, *my* screams.

Fred's hook caught me on the neck and as he was jerking the line trying to free it, he was pulling me along, as I was screaming.

It took him a while to work the hook loose, but after it came out, I mopped up the blood, and felt pretty much okay, and we continued to fish. Well, that's kids for you.

Now there was a certain kind of vine that grew near the pond. We cut the dry, ropy part of the vine into small cigars, lit them up and smoked them. We pretended we were big time fishermen with real stogies. I was a big time *wounded* fisherman with a stogie.

These were lazy days and we were content not catching anything most of the time, but one time we noticed there was another pond on the other side of a fence not too far from where we were fishing.

Somehow we convinced ourselves that this other pond was the one where all the fish were. Big fish, we thought. So we hopped the fence and headed across the private land to the off-limits pond. Who was going to know, anyway? We were a good ways from anywhere.

Well, we were happily fishing when all of a sudden there were rifle shots and kicked-up dirt, and we were dodging real live bullets. I looked up for a second – a pick-up truck was coming at us at top speed, a cloud of dust billowing up behind it, the driver hanging out the window firing at us. The lead was ringing off rocks.

Needless to say, we dropped our home-made rods and scrambled like the old Johnny Horton song says, " . . . We *ran through the brambles and we ran through the bushes where a rabbit couldn't go.*" Off we went, running this way and that, zigging one way, zagging another. Any which-way so as to make a hard target. And although we were each on separate courses, or flights, as you might say, we knew we'd meet on the highway back by the state hospital. But by the time we got there we were muddy from river running. We'd gotten our clothes torn on scrub oaks and brambles and tree cactus, and we were a sight – all ragged and scared and beat half-to-death by running crazy for two miles.

After congratulating ourselves on still being alive, we started walking towards town. For some reason, Tony and I decided to walk across the road. Tony was ahead of me as we crossed. There was a blind spot there where the road went uphill and down, and without warning, a car came flying over that small hill and hit me.

It turned out to be Bob Redding and his wife out for a Sunday drive with their small daughter standing on the front seat between them. The accident might've killed me, but years later I would come to believe it actually saved my life because it kept me from being packed off to Vietnam. I'll come back to this part of the story, but for now . . . let me just say that Mr. Redding was drunk *and* he was traveling on the wrong side of the road. The posted speed limit was 25 mph and Mr. Redding was going 65 when he hit me. He didn't honk or brake before he hit me (no time) as was evident by the absence of skid marks before or after the point of impact.

The collision lifted me four feet in the air, my shoes flew off my feet, I was spun around, and flung onto my stomach facing south, the direction he was headed.

I couldn't move but I could see Mr. Redding disappearing down the highway. I could hear my friends saying, *"Mira – el Joseph esta muerto."* Look – Joseph is dead. He isn't moving.

I lay there on the hot black paved road with blood coming out of my mouth and then I saw Mr. Redding's brake lights blinking. He whipped around in a tight little half-circle, and I thought he was going to roll his car right there, but he came back to where we were – the boys standing there thinking that I was dead.

He asked, "Who's the eldest here?"

Tony said, "I am."

Then Mr. Redding picked me up off the road where I was bleeding and told Tony to get in the back seat with me. Bobby and Carlos were just standing in the road as we went away.

Mr. Redding drove me to the emergency room at the hospital.

As I lay on the back seat, I remember that I was concerned by the way my left foot dangled off the seat. I tried to straighten it some but it wouldn't go that way. The bone was completely broken in half.

I was admitted to the hospital and soon taken into the operating room. My left leg was opened up and a metal plate was attached with screws to the bone to keep it together. I remember being wheeled into a room in a bed. Then, that same day, I was wheeled down the hallway and into the operating room for a second time. Two elderly ladies were sitting on a bench out in the hallway of Saint Anthony's as I went by, and I heard one say, *"That* little boy . . . *again?"*

What had happened was this: the X-Rays indicated the metal plate had moved slightly. My physician, Dr. Terr, now had to open the stitches again, remove the plate, and re-attach it correctly.

Much later, I learned a few more strange facts.

I'd been very lucky, as it turned out. If Mr. Redding's car had struck me above the knee, I probably would've been killed. The doctors surmised this by the speed the car was traveling and the point of impact. There was no certainty, they said, that I'd walk again. When released from the hospital, I left with a giant white cast that went from toe to hip.

My recovery seemed slow – especially to me.

It seemed that even a serious accident where one of his kids almost got killed, didn't help in my dad changing his ways. To some people, an incident like this is a wake up call, but not to him, I guess. For example, there was one day that my father was drunk and in one of his yelling moods. I had been confined to bed for about a month and not able to walk at all. Suddenly my father starts abusing my mother. He pushed her against the wall next to the room where I lay in bed and he was hitting her. All I could do was to force myself into a sitting position and I yelled at him to leave her alone. I saw her hand grab the door way as she was trying to hold herself up. I yelled; *Deja la sola viejo cabron. Leave her alone you son-of-a-bitch.* At that point my mother was able to get away and on her way out the door she grabbed one of the smallest children and ran out the door holding tightly to that baby, whom I can't remember if it was Ereasmo or Jessy. I don't know where everyone else was at.

Well, with mother gone, I was left alone with no one to help me since I was confined to a bed and according to my doctor, that's where I would be for the next two months, which meant all summer.

That afternoon my father also took off so there I was, laying in bed while my dad was out in the bars. No one came home for two days so I didn't eat or drink water for that entire time. At one point, I decided to slide off the bed and attempt to drag myself to the kitchen to find something to eat. I quickly found out this was not possible, because the heavy cast on my leg created too much pressure on my bones to be able to drag myself. The cast was all the way from my toes up to my crotch and it felt as if the bones on my leg were going to be pulled apart, so I somehow lifted myself back onto the bed, and lay there helplessly.

Then in the early evening I heard a car drive up and a woman's voice coming from outside. This person was honking her horn and calling out my sister's name.

Theresa,— Theresa,—-honk, honk, Theresa. I recognized her voice, it was Viola Varela, one of Theresa's friends. I called out to her and I kept yelling until she heard me. I told her to come in and help me, she did. She gave me water and something to eat. I asked her to go to my grandfather's home to see if my mother was there and if she was ok. I knew that's the only place mom could go to.

Finally my dad came home and he was sober by then. He asked me if I knew where my mom had gone to. I didn't tell him until I made him promise me that he wouldn't hit her ever again. Well,—that lasted a short season. Then he drove to pick my mother up at grandpa's.

For months after the accident, I had headaches and spat blood. All I could do was lie in bed and try to rest but that was very difficult. What helped to pass the time away was that Johnny Ortega, a friend of mine, came to visit and he started teaching me how to play the guitar. I would practice and practice the few cords he would teach me each time he came to visit me. But I still kept spitting blood and my leg and insides hurt like hell.

All this time, a local attorney kept telling my father that we had a good lawsuit against the man that hit me, but my father didn't like the attorney, and being the very stubborn man that El Wille could be, he didn't accept the attorney's advice. It turns out we should have gone into litigation so that future medical expenses would be covered. There was concern that I might have internal problems later on in life. Even as it was, I had a permanent limp. To this day, my left leg is a bit shorter than my right. Buying shoes is tricky.

As a juvenile, I had no say in any of this, legally. So, in the end, El Wille accepted a settlement of $900. Of that, I gave $200 each to Mom and El Wille. At that time Juliette, the second eldest daughter was about to get married, so I gave her some money for her wedding. In the end, I kept about $300 for myself. I carried that money in my pocket all summer long.

One of the great pleasures of being "rich" was the I could take my friends to the neighborhood store Julian's, and I treated them to candy, chips and pop. I was popular that summer.

I wore a cast into the start of the next school year as I entered fifth grade. But I got so good with the crutches, that I actually ran races with my friends.

By the way, the attorney's advice (which my stubborn father wouldn't accept), came from the honorable Tiny Martinez.

Now to the part about how the accident saved my life. When I graduated from high school in 1966, I volunteered to join the army. I did this for two reasons: I didn't want to get drafted but I did want to fulfill my duty to my country. The Vietnam war had been on for about three years and I knew I was headed to the front lines during that war.

To this day, I believe that if I'd gone to Vietnam, I'd have died there. It's just a feeling, but a very strong one.

At that same time, I convinced several of my friends to enlist in the army. This way, we might have a choice in the duties available. If drafted, however, there was no choice. Draftees ended up on the front line, from what I'd heard. My friends agreed, we enlisted. The recruiters said at the time of enlistment that we might receive a draft notice in the mail. If we did, we were to take it to them, and that we would possibly have to report a bit earlier for duty. We did get that notice and we were required to report earlier than expected.

During the time I prepared myself for departure, my parents told me to get a letter of release from my doctor. After all, my leg was still a bit of a liability.

However, I never got such a letter, but they did, and on the night before I went to the depot, I saw that letter from my doctor sitting on top of the kitchen table, but I left it there. I didn't want any excuses to impede my enlistment.

So, there we are — me and all my buddies at the recruitment center. The army officers lined us up in a huge, brightly lit room, and then one of them, a sergeant said, "Take off all your clothes."

We did so and then this man stuck a finger into each of our nutsacks, and told us to cough, loud and hard.

Then: "Turn around and bend over!"

At this point, Ray Herrera, who'd always been a clown made some funny joke, which the sergeant didn't take kindly to. We all laughed, but quickly shut our mouths.

While we are all being run through all these procedures in preparation to being sworn in for duty then shipped out the next day, a lady officer, a doctor, came into the room and called out — "Joseph Baca!"

"Yes, ma'am."

"Is it true what it states on the back of your orders . . . about your left leg?"

"Yes, ma'am."

"Step out of line, get dressed and follow me."

"Yes, ma'am."

I remembered that when I filled out all my induction papers about three months earlier, I read on the back side of the last page — any false statements made or withheld personal information, would be held against me in a court of law.

Well, I didn't want to start off on the wrong foot, or rather the wrong leg, so to say, with the armed services, so I had, in fact, written a statement about my accident and my subsequent limp. But no one had bothered to read that last page of my paper work.

So I was taken to a hospital where a recruitment officer and a medical doctor argued why, or why not, they could, or could not, allow me into the Armed Services due to this prior injury to my leg.

In the end, I was told to go home, have the plate removed, wait for my leg to heal, then come back in a year's time; they'd make the decision then.

Well, I went on with my life.

I never did serve in the army.

And I didn't go to Vietnam, though many of my friends did.

Some returned, some didn't.

Some have worse injuries than mine, much worse.

All in all, I believe, as one of my Vietnam-serving buddies said the other day, "You were one lucky fellow."

But it wasn't luck, I don't believe.

Change Of Life,
Change Of Heart

During my middle school and high years, I was unsure how far I'd go in school. Because of the home situation, I had pretty bad study habits or maybe none at all. I mean, how can you concentrate on school work when your life is in danger? I was a C-D-F student for many years while the disharmony and disruption of El Wille turned our home upside down. Still, there was always a part of me that wanted to learn how to be a good student and keep up with the smart kids. Deep down, I didn't believe I belonged with them. Nor was I good enough, in my own personal ranking, to be part of the popular group at school, so I stayed pretty much in the offbeat category of street kid at school only because he has to.

By tenth grade, I wanted to quit school. I'd no interest in furthering my education and I was so far behind in my studies that catching up seemed impossible. I wasn't on track for graduation, and while that bothered me, I had come to accept it as my fate.

But then I started to have a change of heart. I got a job with Job Corps and earned a little money during the summer. My school counselors told me I'd have to attend summer classes for two summers in a row just to catch up with my courses — and that was when I decided to get serious, to start studying and do summer school. Much to my surprise, I enjoyed it. The summer classes were small, the teachers provided one-on-one instruction and I found for the first time that learning wasn't so bad after all. In addition, there weren't any bullies in summer school and so I was free to concentrate and learn at my own pace.

As it turned out, I attended classes for two consecutive summers, one after tenth grade and the next after eleventh. That kept me busy with school work for two full academic years and then the additional two summers. Another big plus — I was so busy I had no time to get into trouble — so I didn't. I still found time to hang around with my regular friends, most of whom I had grown up with, and I also spent some nights with the older guys, too. But, I have to say, even as a studious person, I wasn't offended by older girls and faster cars.

One day while in summer class, we had a visit from the summer school principal. He'd come to introduce himself and get to know his students face-to-face. After he addressed the class, he sat on a desk in front of me. His name was Mr. Arguello and I remember this day well. Right away, Mr. Arguello asked for a volunteer to stand up and explain why we students were there. The class went numb. No one volunteered. Yet with Mr. Arguello sitting right in front of me, I felt obligated to do the honors, so I volunteered.

After my presentation, I returned to my seat.

Mr. Arguello then asked me, "What are you doing here?"

I shrugged, said, "Well, I was flunking school, so I *had* to attend summer school."

He shook his head. "What I mean is, what are you *doing* in summer school?

I explained that ever since junior high I had fallen behind in my school work and then, because I was so far behind, it occurred to me to just drop out and be done with it.

Mr. Arguello nodded. "You have a very nice speaking voice, Joseph," he said, "and your delivery is excellent."

Mr. Arguello, bless his heart, is no longer with us but he is always with me. He couldn't know, at that time, how much his words of encouragement meant. They gave me a reason, a desire to stay in school, so that by my senior year, I had actually fulfilled my required courses. In fact, as a senior I only had two classes left to take. Because of this, I spent my time taking classes I had a special interest in.

My old buddy, Ray Herrera, was in the same place I'd been, two years earlier. He was getting ready to quit. I knew that would be as much of a mistake for him as it was for me, so I paid him a visit. His situation was different than mine though. Ray, after being shot by his cousin, was confined to a wheelchair at that time. The way that happened was, Ray and some friends including his cousin were out shooting guns in the El Creston Mountains west of the city. They were fooling around and Ray got shot in the stomach.

"Don't drop out, Ray," I told him. "You need to finish school. What if I speak to your teachers and get permission to hand deliver your work to you? That way you'll stay on top of your homework, read your texts, and if you keep up, you can finish school at home." Ray said okay and it worked out well for him because, not only did he stay in school, but he graduated the same time I did. I always felt good about visiting him that day and turning his mind toward staying in school instead of dropping out. Today, he's still my good friend and I see him every now and then.

As for the girlfriend, Mitzi, whom I thought I couldn't live without, well, after I almost killed that poor boy, Bobby, her family moved away. However, her parents allowed her to come back to Las Vegas so she could graduate with her classmates. But things were never the same between us and after graduation she moved to Denver and got married.

One night I met Loretta who became the most important person in my life – then and now.

The way it happened, I spoke to Loretta at a dance – we knew each other from school but that was about it – little did I know how this one little encounter was going to change my life.

That first meeting was at a place called The Blue Light City. It was the place where teens gathered for dances. At the time I used to work with a friend, Bobby Ortiz, who had a photography business. We used to take pictures of the teen dancers. I was a senior in high school then; Loretta had graduated the year before, 1965.

Anyway, strange to say, Loretta didn't like me very much at the time, and, honestly, I didn't feel attracted to her either. But we gave it a try – we started dating. It wasn't long before I was spending all of my spare time with her. She stopped hanging around with her girlfriends, and a strong bond developed between us so that, after a while we were inseparable.

Getting To Know Loretta

While working with my friend, Bobby Ortiz at his photography studio, I got into developing and printing wedding pictures and other social events that I caught with my camera – this was good experience and one that I still use.

As I mentioned earlier, it was during this time, photographing dancers with Bobby that I met Loretta Sedillo, but what I haven't said is that I had had a plan, a program, if you will, and that was to avoid any deep relationships, to play the field as we used to say.

Well, there went my plan . . . I got so serious about Loretta that I stopped seeing any other girls and I gave up my guy friends as well. No more cool older guys with their quicker liquor, faster women and high-speed cars.

While we were dating, Loretta worked at the New Mexico State Hospital which was not far from town. She owned a white 1957 Chevy Impala which I kept during the day so I could work on it – I got new seat covers and had the engine worked on by my friends. In the afternoon, when her shift was over, I drove out to the State Hospital and picked up Loretta. When she worked nights, I picked her up in the early hours. I spent more and more time at her house – sometimes even when she wasn't there. When I wasn't working, for instance, I helped her father with his chores: chopping wood, yard work, whatever. I was really there waiting for her but there was a genuine tie to her family that I began to accept as something I'd missed having at my own home.

There were many things that drew me to Loretta but perhaps one of the most important was that, when we were together, I discovered I could talk to her about anything: my past, my present, my future. This added to the bond that was forming between us. I'd never had anyone I could confide in so completely, no one I could trust so deeply that, no matter what I said, they'd be listening and not judging. This was something I really cherished in Loretta – quiet patience and understanding.

Because we'd been schoolmates, Loretta already knew a few things about my past. She knew a lot about the girlfriend I'd dated from junior high through high school. She knew about the boy I'd stabbed over this former girl of mine. But my uncertain past, full of pain and sorrow, my present, with all of its indecisions, these didn't put Loretta off and I found acceptance in her that I'd missed during the turbulent and crazy years with El Wille running our lives.

In Loretta, I was always safe. If I wanted to talk about the hurt that had hardened my heart when I was young, she listened. If I wanted to speak of my father's brutality, she listened. What an amazing thing that is — for someone who's never had it. How healing it is to be able to express things that are locked up inside you and that you fear to release because of censure.

As time went on (and like many others in our community) I too found a job at the State Hospital working the day shift. As a result, Loretta and I would sometimes be off work at the same time. So we started spending almost all of our time together, and for a while, we used to go dancing with friends in the evenings and generally having a good time whenever we could.

Eventually though this partying seemed to lose its luster and it finally came to an end when Loretta and I started reading the Bible together. We were discovering that both of us shared an inner hunger to know and understand more about God, religion, and about our true purpose in this world. I'd always wondered about this and now I discovered that both of us sought spiritual rejuvenation.

At the same time, we couldn't seem to find any solace in the Catholic faith we were raised in; that set us apart from most young people our age who were, one way or another, culturally sealed by the old ways of the Catholic Church.

While reading of other religions and beliefs, we discovered a small church on Hot Springs Boulevard where we were finally baptized in water and brought into yet another fold of devoutly religious people.

Of course, this didn't mean we'd become monks or anything like that. We still had our life, and we were young enough to enjoy it. Often we'd drive around town in Loretta's white Chevy Impala listening to the music on Las Vegas's own KFUN radio station. At night too we tuned into KOMA out of Oklahoma, and listened to the good Rock-N-Roll sounds of Wolf Man Jack.

Loretta's car was, truth to say, pretty hot. It really stood out in town with the red stripe accented with chrome the entire length of the chassis. The long, shapely fins in back looked fantastic and I'd installed mag pipes which were not as loud as they were rumbly, and we used to park at the A & W drive-in and enjoy some burgers and fries and root beer sodas. After that, crank up the engine, step on the gas pedal and let those pipes grumble and growl. In that way, we'd let everyone know that Loretta and Joseph were in town. Harmless fun, really, when I think back on it. And what did it cost? Almost nothing. Then again, nothing *was* nothing back then.

Then a change I wasn't expecting . . .

Loretta's step sister, her husband and their children lived in Huachuca City, Arizona. The entire family was into religion and Bible study, prayer meetings and revivals, and this appealed to both of us.

Loretta desired a change, so she decided to move to Arizona and be with her step-sister.

Well, what was I going to do without Loretta?

I couldn't see myself living in Las Vegas, alone. Not after I'd been with her and she'd helped straighten my life out. Besides, the town would've been empty without her. The streets would turn mighty lonely for me, so I just packed up and went along with her.

In Arizona, we met all kinds of different people. There were plenty of folks who believed in alternate religions in Huachuca City and we started attending churches of all kinds while reading books that offered philosophies totally unknown in my parent's world. God and the spirit of holiness was within not without, and we quickly found that form and function in religion were two entirely different things.

We attended services at a college called Miracle Valley. The church leader and founder was Sam Fife. Sam was a charismatic preacher who delivered sermons in clothes that would've delighted Liberace. As it turned out, Sam led a kind of double life. He sermonized abstinence and demonized selfishness, but he lived in a huge mansion, had a great hexagonal swimming pool, and he liked to skinny dip with young, pretty female followers. This pastime, in fact, cost him his ministry.

However, truth be known, Reverend Fife is but one of many ministers who brought themselves down with their own misconduct and secret shame all during the sixties. These were men whose darker lives were hidden from view while their persona at the pulpit was self-righteous, self-sacrificing and so misleading.

Anyway the Reverend didn't keep Loretta and me from seeking other churches and other ways of thinking about religion. The only problem was, I think we were looking for answers in other people. It would take some years before we found the spiritual meaning of life we were looking for, and then it wouldn't come from others but from deep within ourselves.

We continued to live in Huachuca City and I worked in Tucson and drove fifty miles each way to work every day. This got tiring so we decided to move to Tucson. Living there, we met people who had prayer meetings in their homes and these were steady folks and we attended their meetings often. Our hunger for books helped us and so did our inquiring minds and the good people we spent time with who were much the same, full of heart.

As Loretta and I continued studying the Bible and learned more about other spiritual leaders from around the world, we started to experience what I might call a kind of "spiritual awakening." I use quotes here because that can be misunderstood as "spiritual arrival."

We were initiates and we read many self-help books by different authors, but the more we read, the more we learned and the more we learned, the more we yearned for a true spiritual birth.

For the first time in my life, I was starting to connect with my inner world, little lost boy I'd left behind in Las Vegas, sitting on a bench at the Plaza Park, crying his heart out.

Ever so gently, an awareness came into my mind. This was nothing more and nothing less than a willingness to admit that until I was willing to recognize my own inner weaknesses, I would not and could not change myself.

The time had finally come for me to stop pampering that little lost boy within and start nourishing my essentially strong, spiritual being. Thus I started facing my personal fears about life and my inexperience in relating to other people. I began to see that my negative feelings towards my father had grown into a kind of blind hatred, and that this was something I'd harbored, even nurtured since I was very young.

With that realization, I progressed even further. I remembered the protective force that had kept me from harm, possibly from early death, when I was a boy. Now I was feeling this spirit within as never before, and it was showing me a better way. It was time to grow up and become the productive human being I was meant to be. It was time for the demons to meet the spiritual me.

I was still afraid though and I knew I couldn't walk this unknown path by myself. There were too many demons on this dirt road waiting to keep me from going forward. I knew it would take many years of dedicated soul searching to overcome my personal weaknesses.

True to form, I found a friend in Loretta. She was there as before to support me and offer encouragement and spiritual insight in conquering my inner demons.

The truth was that my childhood was following me into my adulthood, and unknowingly, but surely, I'd already started to subject Loretta to the El Willé that dwelt within. I knew that I could not be a good friend, lover, and in time, supporting husband, if I did not change now. I could still fulfill my father's angry prophecy — "You'll never be worth a damn and you'll never accomplish anything in life!" God help me, it could go either way, and as I recognized the darkness of this curse, I knew I needed the light of that other wisdom, the protective force that had saved me when I was young.

I took the first step on February 25, 1967. That was the day I began my new life, the day Loretta and I got married in Tucson, Arizona.

Different Kinds Of Spanish

The sun was bright and hot in Arizona and Loretta and I were together again. It took me a while to find a job, but Loretta found one right away. I kept looking and I finally got a call from a carpet store that wanted to interview me. The owner, Orlando Sotomayor came from Mexico City, and he liked that I spoke Spanish, albeit New Mexico style, so I was hired.

My first day on the job, I didn't know exactly what I'd be doing; I was just told to report at 9: a. m. However, as I wanted to make the right impression on my first day, and as I imagined I'd be in sales, I showed up in dress slacks, white shirt and tie. On arrival I was taken to Fry Boulevard and we walked into a warehouse where I was introduced to my instructor, Gàbriel Martinez, a native of Agua Prieta, Mexico, just across the border from Douglas, Arizona.

I was given a very large needle and some thread. Gábriel told me to sit on the floor, and he instructed me in the art of sewing a binding on the edge of a carpet. I felt foolish in my dress pants, white shirt and tie, learning the ancient art of hand sewing and carpet binding – and, oh, did my fingers hurt after a few hours of needling.

All things considered though, I loved my new job. Installing carpets was hard work but it also kept me in top shape. Gábriel was a talented artisan from the old school, and besides knowing carpets, he was also an expert at upholstery. He spoke no English.

When we went into a home to install a carpet, the first thing Gábriel did was check out the furniture. If it looked old and worn out, he'd use me as his interpreter to convince the home owner to hire him as an upholsterer. Often he'd pick up old discarded furniture from some of the homes where we were installing carpet. Then he'd reupholster it and make it look new. Later these pieces sold at a handsome profit to him, but one that was nonetheless a bargain for the home owner.

Gábriel offered to teach me the upholstery business but I never took him up on it – what a mistake that was because upholstery and carpet installation go hand-in-hand, and I could have learned not one, but two valuable skills at the same time.

For the first few months we worked together, my northern New Mexico old world Spanish didn't quite meet up with Gabriel's borderland Mexico dialect. It took some months before he would ask for a certain tool, and I'd hand him the right one. When I gave him the wrong tool, he'd shake his head, smile, say the word again. Fortunately, we got along fine and once we overcame the language barrier, we were in perfect sync.

Sometimes though we ran into difficulties.

Like when Loretta was working in McClellan's department store, which was much like a mini version of Wal-Mart, and Gábriel and I were working in a newly constructed home installing carpet and I asked him, *"Gábriel, usa tu esposa pantalones?"* Gábriel, does your wife use pants?

I asked this because I wanted to tell him that the store where Loretta worked was having a big sale on women's clothing.

But Gábriel just gave me a hard look and said darkly, "Que me proguntas? Como que si mi esposa usa pantalones?"

After a little cross-examination, he discovered my innocence in the matter. In *my* Spanish, *pantalones* means *pants*. But in *his* Spanish, it means *panties*. No wonder he raised his eyebrows.

Well, we eventually had a good laugh over this one. But there were many more situations like this where words got the better or brought out the worst in us. One way or the other, I guess it's true what the poet Carl Sandburg once said about words, that they walk off proud and can't hear you calling.

Michel

There is a part of our lives that Loretta and I have shared with a few of her family members, as well as mine. Now I share it with whoever reads this book. We consider this part of our personal life, something sacred and not spoken about publicly. Why do I share it now? The former belief that no one would believe us is no longer important. Besides, there's nothing to prove nor to boast about, nothing to gain, nothing to keep secret.

One Sunday while we were living in Tucson, we attended a prayer meeting in a private home. The woman of the house was a visionary who had visions and offered prophesies. On that day, she looked at Loretta and told her that she was carrying a child, a boy.

We'd been trying to have a child for some time and this was confirmation, but we didn't know what to think of the woman's prophecy. After all, we didn't know her; she was a stranger to us. But, somehow, we felt the truth of what she said, and Loretta, trusting her inner voice went home and started making baby clothing for a boy. Shortly after this, we visited our obstetrician and he confirmed that Loretta was with child, and indeed it was a boy.

This was confirmation of our spiritual trust in the higher power that surrounded us with light. We were overjoyed that we'd soon add a son to our small family. During this time we got close to another couple, Charlie and Nonine Anderson, who were also expecting a child. Nonine's due date was a few months before Loretta's. The friendship with other believers was helpful and reassuring for all four of us.

In addition, there was yet another couple, Andrew and Mary Jacobson, both retired doctors and ordained ministers who attended our prayer meetings. This couple had devoted their lives to working in Mexico, giving professional medical help to families without means to see a doctor. As we got to know them better, we told them that we were expecting our first born. This took effort on my part because, at that time, I seldom trusted new acquaintances enough to reveal our personal lives to them. Yet as we got to know this elderly couple, Loretta and I found we could really open our hearts and trust them.

As doctors, they had strong beliefs based on their experience with childbirth. This was knowledge practiced and taught to expectant mothers and fathers in Mexico. First, they believed that the man had to take responsibility for impregnating the mother. They required the man to be involved in helping to bring the child into the world from start to finish. At the time of delivery, the man was supposed to squat behind his wife and place his arms around her upper stomach and apply gentle downward pressure as the expectant mother also squatted with her arms on top of her husband's thighs very close to his knees. Using him as support, she was then more capable of pushing with her abdomen in a downward motion.

Our new friends and confidants were well-qualified as experts of the human body, especially a woman's body during and after childbirth. Birthing on the back, typical hospital style, they believed was not the best way for a woman to prepare for giving birth. In their belief this relaxed way of birthing, effective in its own way, was not the best because it didn't utilize a woman's natural strength as much as squatting did.

Andrew and Mary explained that when a woman is squatting, she can feel her body – legs, back, spine – supporting her and this position firms the abdomen and stomach muscles, naturally and freely, so they can begin to move in a downward motion.

The doctors also emphasized that it's also important for the woman to be on her tip-toes, rather than flat-footed on the floor, when using the squat delivery method. In this way, the downward motion is gravitational and it allows the fetus to slide out of the womb.

Another blessing came our way. Friends of ours, Jackie and Carl Peterson, offered us their large camper trailer to live in while we waited for the birth of our son. By accepting their generous offer, we would be saving an additional $500 dollars a month. Such a saving might really help with our planned move back to New Mexico after our son was born.

The only question was, where to park the travel trailer. Our friends Nonine and Charlie lived in a large Spanish style home that used to be a museum and sat on a large piece of property. It was close to a Sears store and shopping malls for ease of shopping. They invited us to park the trailer on their property and permitted us to string a long extension cord from their home for electric hook up.

This was a perfect setup, and so there we were, living in this cozy camper under the Arizona sky. Under the bright desert moon, we also had the solitary, peaceful company of tall saguaro cactus that stood against the sky like a guardian.

Perfection sometimes demands attention. That is, attention to detail. The camper was comfortable with a stove, refrigerator, table, two bedrooms, a bathroom and plenty of closet space. But the dining table was the folding type, which was supported by one leg when in use. One evening we sat down for a delicious supper that Loretta had prepared. Beans, fried potatoes, red chili, a fresh salad with tortillas and desert. *Sounds like a meal my dear mother used to prepare.*

I got up from the table to get something, and while sliding out of my seat, I knocked the single supporting leg out from under the table – and our fabulous meal, plates and all came crashing to the floor. There we were, food all over us, laughing. I thought, *Maybe our newborn thinks it's funny too!*

Time passed, and as we got closer to Loretta's due date, we discussed the thought of Loretta doing a natural birth at home with me assisting the delivery. Our good friends Nonine and Charlie had decided to do it this way and so we talked together about assisting each other with our mutual deliveries. Of course, the doctors would also be present.

Finally it came time for Nonine to have her baby and Charlie was prepared to do the delivery with Loretta and I standing by to assist. All went well with the birth of their baby with no problems. I was surprised how quick it all happened for Nonine. But of course, she had given birth before so I guess this facilitated this birth. That night after the delivery of their child, Charlie and I walked outside to bury the placenta deep enough in the desert so animals wouldn't smell it and dig it up, which is what the doctors instructed us to do. Next day, Charlie took Nonine and their baby for a doctor's medical checkup and all was well with both.

Meantime, Loretta's delivery date kept approaching and we were mentally prepared for this blessed experience. One thought that was creating some pressure for me was that Loretta's mother would be traveling to Tucson to be with her during the delivery. This made it tough for me – that my mother-in-law would be present while her daughter would be having her first child, with her crazy son-in-law performing the delivery.

Since I would be delivering our son, I couldn't be positioning myself behind Loretta, so I devised a stool for her to sit on during the delivery. I took a new toilet seat, cut six inches off the front on each side, bought a small bar stool, took the seat off and cut the metal legs short enough so the birthing stool would be about eight inches off the floor. I then attached the frame to the toilet seat, and there is where Loretta would sit for the delivery.

We had totally cleaned and sanitized the room which would serve as the delivery area. Finally, Loretta's water broke and we were all ready for the delivery. Our doctor friends were right there with us following my every move and with a gentle hand on my shoulder as a sign of support.

Because this was Loretta's first child the delivery process took longer than usual, but the doctors reassured us all was well. Keep in mind that all through this delivery process, my mother-in-law was sitting in the next room next to the doorway listening to every little detail. The fear I must have put her through! But she never said a word. She just kept working on a small blanket she'd been sewing for her new grandson. (Incidentally, our son, now 41 years old, still has that small blanket.)

Then, quickly, the baby's head appeared, then his shoulders, then his entire body. Our son was born. However, I noticed the umbilical cord was wrapped around the newborn's neck. I stayed calm and did as our doctor friends had instructed me. I removed the cord from his neck, placed one hand on his heels, the other on his neck, and then I began working his little body like an accordion, back and forth, until he started crying loudly, which only took a second. Later, Loretta and I joked that our son cried like a little donkey.

I followed all the proper steps, placed two fingers on Loretta's stomach by the umbilical cord, tied it above my fingers real tight, cut the cord and handed the baby to our doctors for a complete inspection. All was fine with the baby and Loretta was well but very exhausted. We put both to bed for the night, fed Loretta plenty of liquids, and kept them warm. Next day I took mom and baby to our regular doctor for a full physical checkup. Thankfully all was well.

We hadn't chosen a name for our son because we wanted it to be a special name. So for two weeks, our son was unnamed. There we were peacefully living in the small trailer under the Arizona sky.

One morning, Loretta asked me how the name Michael was spelled. I spelled it for her. She told me she had a dream the night before about Michael the Archangel. She'd been asking God to reveal the name of our newborn. She said, "God is not a good speller." In her dream, she saw the name Michael written in flames, but spelled *Michel*. We held onto this, believing it to be our son's true name.

One day while we were attending a prayer meeting, a singer sang a song he said he'd just written. The song was about Michael the Archangel. The lyrics went as follows: *Michael the Archangel was in the flames and the flame was Michael the Archangel.*

Loretta and I accepted this as yet another spiritual affirmation.

New Mexico Joys And Blues

In 1969 while living in Tucson we rented a large U-Haul truck, packed it with our belongings and headed for New Mexico. Our son Michel who was less than a month old was sleeping in a baby carrier and here we were heading home with a newborn and a new idea.

We visited with my in-laws, first, and then my parents in Las Vegas. We wanted the family to see Michel and get to know him a little bit before we drove on to Albuquerque which was our destination. There we found a small home to rent while I explored the new territory. What I was going to do was an extension of what I'd already done in Tucson, but here in Albuquerque the growth potential was expanding.

For a while I worked for a company that installed floor covering – ceramic and Mexican tile – in the development known as Rio Rancho. When I first saw the area, all vacant and, to me, unattractive, I wondered why anyone would want to live in a giant sand box outside of Albuquerque?

The answer lay partly in the presentation of Ramco, the New York developer who was flying in prospective buyers from the East. Potential clients, dreaming of starting a new life, or retiring from an old one, came to the sunbelt with great eagerness. What they saw was perhaps a little different than my own version of the place. For them, this was the sunny and expansive Land of Enchantment. The Ramco pitch did the rest. Part of that sales pitch was that if someone bought a home, the company paid their moving expenses on completion of the building.

Not all of these home buyers were pleased once they moved in. Rio Rancho had been arid undeveloped land since the conquistadores saw it and it was likely that when the windy season hit, the dust would fly off the level plains and be quite a nuisance. As it happened, front lawns actually got buried under a foot of sand.

There were other things to contend with as well. Yes, it was sunny most of the time, but in winter it was cold and in summer it was very hot. Ramco believed, however, that Rio Rancho was going to grow so large that it would eventually link up with Paradise Hills in the south and Bernalillo to the North.

The employees of the company I worked for didn't believe a word of the Ramco hype, but on the other hand if it were even remotely true, we'd all have work for some time to come. So we generally refrained from knocking the expansion theory.

On Fridays, Loretta would pick me up after work, and we drove to Las Vegas to visit our families. This was our weekend routine, and a great pleasure to us, because for a long time we'd been isolated from family members while living in Arizona. It wasn't long before Loretta got pregnant with our second child, which I welcomed with joy because I'd always wanted a big family, twelve, to be exact. (What was I thinking?) Anyway, she gave birth to a little girl whom we named Annette Margaret Baca. *Margaret, after my dear mother.* A little beauty with light skin and blond hair. And what a talkative girl she became as time went on, outgoing and pretty. She also demanded lots of attention as she grew up, but now I'm getting ahead of myself.

There were many happy times with Michel and Annette. We lived in a Spanish style home with half round arches in the front and a flat roof which of course is popular and practical in New Mexico. We lived on the corner of Central and Wellesly, right behind Baca's Restaurant – same name, no relation.

Loretta worked at the carry-out section of Baca's for a while, which was nice because employees were allowed to bring home Mexican food.

We used to spend lots of time with our children taking them for walks in a stroller, playing at the park. I would take Michel out on his small bike so he could learn to ride it. Playing with the kids out in our very large back yard was a special family time.

Shady Lakes was a family type camping ground where small children could fish without a license. You paid a nominal fee for each fish caught. Michel and Annette really enjoyed this and it was fun to see their excitement when they had a live fish on the line. Looking back, these were all joyous times.

I remember we once bought each of them a small rabbit to play with. Quickly, two became four, then six, and after a while we had a family of small rabbits running loose in our back yard. We didn't like to keep them caged. Besides, our back yard was enclosed with a tall brick wall and the bunnies couldn't get out. But in time they dug holes all around the yard and made an underground warren where they lived. Yet they still trusted us and would come up and eat carrots out of our hands.

Rabbit running and catching was a special, fun-filled sport for our family. The kids and I would leap into the air ready to grab a rabbit, but the rabbits were only teasing us by sitting still, and just when we were about to grab one, they'd disappear into one of their many holes.

Our house had a large picture window facing east. In the dining room we had an amazing view of the Sandia Mountains. We enjoyed the beautiful sunrise with the turquoise New Mexico sky, and during the month of September, we'd open the drapes very early in the morning to see the Albuquerque airways full of colorful hot air balloons. This was during the Balloon Fiesta at the State Fair grounds, which were about a half mile east of us.

We would take the kids there to see the inflating of the balloons. I remember holding Michel in my arms one time when we stood underneath a large globe looking straight up into its depths. It frightened Michel and he held me tightly as I laughed. We walked from globe to globe as each was being inflated and you saw the primary colors unfolding, and then you'd hear the roar of the burners giving the balloons the lift they needed to slowly rise up into the blue New Mexico sky, and then away they went.

Attending the State Fair with our children was another exciting event. We mostly walked around visiting the exhibits, especially those with animals for the kids to see and pet. Occasionally I took the kids swimming at a nearby public pool. They swam while I played around with them in the water. I was a good doggy-paddler, but after my experience at Storrie Lake I was always cautious around water.

I stayed in the carpet business and enjoyed it. I took my job seriously, never skipped work, and was always on time. My boss appreciated this dedication, but my co-workers poked fun because of a certain work ritual I practiced.

Carpet installation is very physical and demanding in that it requires a lot of constant lifting of heavy rolls of carpet, moving furniture. Also you're kneeling and your pants wear out at the knees. I didn't like looking sloppy, so I had an assortment of jumpsuits that I wore to work. Before I began to work, I asked the homeowner's permission to use their bathroom where I removed my clean jumpsuit and changed into my work clothes.

After the job was done, I switched back into my jumpsuit, combed my hair and cleaned up a bit. After that, I was ready for our next installation. The guys I worked with weren't as fastidious as I was, and maybe they didn't smell as nice, but they'd make fun of me every time – "Hold it, guys, we can't start the job until Joseph changes into his work clothes." Then after the job was finished, someone said, "Hold it, guys, we can't leave for our next job until Joseph changes back to Mr. Clean." I didn't mind the jokes. Besides, my neatness *was* appreciated by the customers, and that was what mattered most.

Another ritual I practiced: I always put a clean piece of carpet on the homeowner's kitchen floor. On top of this, I put my tool box, then my tools. The reason behind this – I didn't want to risk scratching a new kitchen floor. Eventually, these little things got back to my boss, who heard customers say that I was neat, professional, and polite.

I liked hearing that my methods set a high standard, but honestly, being a carpet layer (and working for someone else) wasn't really what I envisioned as my goal in life. I wanted to own my own carpet store, be my own boss, but that seemed to be like an untouchable dream most of the time, although, some of the time I believed it was possible. My life had been like that, moving up from nothing to something. What was the next something?

Without our really knowing it, there were changes taking place in our life, and Loretta and I started feeling them. It was like a dark wind was blowing across the empty spaces and catching us when we weren't looking.

Maybe it would've felt different if we'd been attending church but, for some reason, we couldn't seem to find a church we liked. We'd also lost interest in attending home meetings like the ones in Tucson. I began to see things in myself that I didn't like but felt helpless to fix. After work I drank beer with some of my co-workers and I hung out in bars with them when I should've been at home.

This self-destructive behavior, given my background with El Wille, got on Loretta's nerves quickly. I wasn't coming home in time for dinner and when I did return, we got into arguments about my staying out late and drinking. My life was unraveling and I couldn't stop the dysfunction. Worst of all, there was a separation between Loretta and me, and though it bothered me, I was unable to prevent it from happening. The dark wind of emptiness was haunting me and hurting me and my family, and on some level, I knew where the wind was from – it came from my dark past and from the beatings I endured as a kid.

I knew this as much as I knew how much it was harming Loretta, Michel and Annette, but I couldn't, or wouldn't, change the direction I was going, the free-fall into the nightmare of El Wille.

In the end, I didn't fight it.

I let the dark wind carry me away, carry me back.

Looking at it now, it's understandable that, as they say, we treat others as we have been treated. I was now treating myself the way El Wille had treated me, but there was an undertow of anger in me, still unresolved feeling of former times when one minute you were safe and the next minute your life was in danger.

Some time passed, and then I was yelling at Loretta, staring her down like El Wille Moto. In fact, sometimes, glancing in the mirror, I saw him — his face, only now it was mine. Such rage burned behind my eyelids.

I actually wondered if this ghost of the past was inhabiting me to such a degree that I was becoming El Wille. Nightmares of the old chalupa, the Pontiac head glowing in the dark.

Things got so bad in our relationship that one day I lashed out at my Loretta and struck her. This, I am ashamed to say, happened more than once. She'd leave the house and I'd beg her to come back home.

There were moments of blinding clarity when I witnessed myself, the person I'd come to be, and I saw the way I stood, the way I fumed and raged, and I knew the demon was back but I couldn't confront him — he had too much power.

Time would pass as it must, as it does for everyone.

And healing, a little here, a little there, happened.

It wasn't enough, but it *was* something.

And then things would get better for a while, and we'd be happy again and getting along as husband and wife. But this wouldn't last for long. One day I watched Loretta shopping and tending to our children. I was there with her, helping, doing my best to be there. But a large part of me was elsewhere. At once I felt shut out of Loretta's life. She was busy, she was well, she was doing what she was supposed to be doing. I was there with her, but as I say, I wasn't there at the same time. I was lost and alone in the cold dark wind of the bad days of my childhood.

On the other hand, there were times when I felt I was a good husband and father. I used to help Loretta with bathing the children and changing their dirty dippers. Sometimes some of my sisters would visit us and find me rinsing diapers in the toilet getting them ready for washing. They would tease me, saying,

"You're going to get dishpan hands, Joseph." Actually, I liked cleaning house and washing dishes and diapers as I found this activity comforting and relaxing, a time to heal my mind, or try to anyway.

As I began to get a grip on my life again, it occurred to me that there were yet other problems I had to face. For example, when I was functioning quite well, I felt myself diminished in some way that I couldn't explain. The excitement Loretta and I had always had being together seemed to have worn off. Maybe my hanging out with friends and drinking after work and being absent in my marriage and family life was affecting me more than I knew. Maybe it also had something to do with just being bored or not being able to visualize my next goal in life. Maybe I felt that Loretta was devoting all her time to the kids, and I was being neglected. Neglect can lead to loss, and loss can lead to sorrow and anger. These were the places where I had been long ago, trapped in isolation. Longing for love. Being so alone, no one could reach me.

How stupid and childish of me not to figure this out more quickly. But you must remember the power of the past. The way it holds you with roots that go deep into the dark earth of unremembered days and hours. It's the times you forget that haunt you the most.

In a clear state of mind, I should've seen that Loretta wasn't neglecting me, she was simply being a mother, and a good one at that. Through all of this though, one thing we always did was talk. And that talk was healing. This was the thing in Loretta that drew me to her in the first place. At night, we'd lay in bed sharing our feelings about our lives, our relationship, the unraveling, and I would tell her again what it was like growing up in a world of constant fear.

Our conversation was often about God, religion and our desire to find the meaning of our lives. We shared the same yearning to know the meaning of the universe. We knew there was more to life than what we saw on the linear plane of mere existence. We realized that we were spiritual beings living in a physical world. But I wanted to know more, and so did she. I wanted to experience Loretta's inner being, her true spirit, and she wanted to experience mine.

Now more than ever, we continued searching and reading self-help books and sometimes when a preacher came through town, we'd attend his service and listen to him preach.

I remember one preacher that came through Albuquerque, he was preaching at a coliseum off I-25. The place was packed from the first bleachers at the floor level to the last bleachers at the top by the entrance.

On this day, the evangelist spoke in his polished preacher voice. "Dear Jesus, send your spirit upon this gathering and heal the sick and afflicted, HAL-LA-LU-YAH, use me as your instrument here today."

Some fancy preachers use all sorts of gimmicks to get their audience to buy into their sermon. *They plant their followers* in amongst the crowds. They have the one that repeats, HAL-A-LU-YAH every time the preacher shouts this out. Then there is the dancer. That's the one that takes off dancing down the isles with hands high in the air. The one that speaks in some strange language. They call it, *speaking in* tongues. Finally, the big event. The show would not be complete without that one follower that pro-*claims, or fakes* a healing.

Don't misunderstand me. It's not that I don't believe in these miracles. But, in many prayer revivals, I have seen many staged religious *exhibitions* that some televangelists pass off as miracles.

So, back to the preacher. Here was this young preacher, prancing and dancing and dressed to kill, pacing up and down the stage like a peacock, boasting about his personal knowledge of God's word.

Then something funny happened. Some guy in the audience challenged the preacher and he was yelling at the top of his voice telling the big man that he was misquoting the passages in the Bible. You can imagine how much this upset the preacher. *How dare this simple peasant of a man question and challenge me and my ministry?* It got so bad that the minister jumped from the stage, ran out to the floor, and started yelling through the open microphone at this guy. But, the challenger stood his ground and fired angry words back at the preacher. Suddenly, the preacher dashed up into the bleachers, knocked people out of his way, and got into a fist fight with the heckler.

The funny part happened when the preacher used his microphone as a club to hit the guy over the head. As he hit him, over and over, you could hear *thunk-thump, thunk–thump* reverberating throughout the whole auditorium and that was when I told Loretta, "Let's get out of here, I don't want our kids exposed to this."

This was perhaps an important turning point of our spiritual life. We realized that our world, the real world was within *and* without, but you didn't need to search for it outside yourself; it would come to you, if you were patient, and we decided right there that we'd be more patient with ourselves and more aware of what was going on around us.

Our family was about to get a little larger. Loretta was pregnant again and we were expecting a third baby. In preparing for the birth we decided to have the delivery in Las Vegas at Loretta's sister's home.

Joseph P. Baca Jr. was born on March 6, 1975. Loretta had the baby by natural birth and was assisted by Doña Jesusíta, an amazing midwife who during her career would deliver more than 4,000 babies.

Michel was now six years old and I wanted him to experience this wonder of life, and to see the birth. So, I brought Michel into the bedroom where the delivery was to take place and I stood him at the foot of the bed, and he witnessed his little brother being born.

Our daily lives went on with the same routine of work and survival. And then, at the same time, we each started talking about moving again. I wanted to move back to Las Vegas but Loretta didn't warm up to this idea. She said I still had too many old friends and bad old memories there, and this wouldn't be good for my head or for our marriage. I knew she was right and I gave up on the idea of moving to Las Vegas, but we both felt a move coming into our lives. One did, and it happened just after Joseph Jr. was born.

Snohomish
(Secrets in the Shadows)

Our move to Snohomish, Washington State was positive in a number of ways.

First and foremost, Loretta and I liked the spiritual friendships we formed with many of the families and our lives were very busy with the daily management of our carpet business.

This is a photo of Loretta and me standing in front of our business,
A-I Carpet and Floor Covering as evident by our business sign behind us.

Joseph & Loretta. The young boy is J. R. Baca (Joseph), our youngest son. Today J. R. is an employee of the family business, KFUN/AM 1230 & KLVF/FM 100.7.

This is a photo of me, Loretta and our son Joseph Jr. inside our carpet store.

Eden Farms was a place where the youth learned about tilling the ground, planting gardens and harvesting the fruits of their labor. But as good as this was, there was a dark side to Eden Farms lurking in the shadows. Something I felt more than witnessed — at least in the beginning.

There were two organizations, Eden Farms and Ellogos. Religion and business went hand in hand here, and I guess this overall organization could be called a commune. Something like the famous transcendental Brook Farm back in the 19th century.

There were many buildings on the property. A bunk house where the teenage boys lived under the watchful eye of a housemother. These boys tended to livestock, horses, pigs, and other animals that roamed the lush meadows of Eden Farms . They worked the land with tractors, trucks and farm equipment.

Ellogos consisted of business professionals like Dr. Howard Morse, CPA's business consultants and business owners who were electricians, plumbers, carpenters, teachers, two horticulturists that conducted classes for the youth along with caring for the vineyards and gardens while managing Eden Farms' nursery, one of the many businesses co-owned by Craig Reynolds and Ted Renaldo. Eden Farms contained about four homes with the biggest one belonging to the big man, Ted Renaldo.

Tom Metcalf, a retired professional horse trainer in his seventies was known nationwide in the horse racing and breeding industry. He served in judging professional show horses, gave riding lessons for which Eden Farms charged prices ranging in the thousands.

Ted was also the owner and editor of two small tabloid newspapers. He and a staff of women managed these. All of the commune's business ventures were expanding rapidly and new ones were being added every few years. The fast growth of companies and their expansion into the local economy surprised and concerned the townspeople of Snohomish. Soon there was a lot of gossip going around. The locals were wondering – Who are these people? Where have they come from, and where are they getting their money for starting so many new businesses?

Ted and the business leaders of the group were the driving force behind the businesses. I think Ted wanted to be the head of the business ventures because he could then claim half ownership, but one business escaped him – our own carpet store. We made sure of that.

There were so many businesses that I don't think I can remember them all. But let me try. The horse farm, the horse breeding services , the wholesale nursery, the retail nursery, the flower shop, Eden Farms Landscaping, (in a lush state like Washington, this was big business) and the newspapers. There was also a day care and pre-school for the younger children of the Eden Farms' family. All families paid for the day care services. Also Ted opened an exclusive art gallery in Snohomish called Golden Gallery. He purchased three homes, one in Everett and two in Snohomish; and an elderly religious follower, *Eloise,* added Ted to her will and left her home to him.

In addition, there was the elaborate tourist mansion, Tallotam, the large tourist lodge that sat right next to the Snoqualmie River situated in a green, lush wooded area East of Snohomish. Tallotam was a three story building with thirteen separate rooms including living quarters, a large commercial kitchen, a huge living and dining room to entertain guests, a big indoor swimming pool and many outdoor patios. Tallotam drew big income for Ellogos, which really meant, large amounts of cash into Ted's personal account. Money given to Ellogos, the religious arm of the organization, in my opinion, most likely also landed up in some special account listed under Ted's name. Religious followers are generous people if they believe in their leader.

Ted was a forward-thinking entrepreneur and this was mostly the quality in him that drew me to him, plus his charisma and the way he won people over. I believed I could learn from him but he always wanted things done his way. He bristled when challenged by anyone, so he and I locked horns quite often. Because I wouldn't play his way, Ted never really trusted me — yet the feeling was mutual. I couldn't trust him either, and I think he knew this.

There seemed to be no end to Ted's enthusiasm and talent. He was gifted musically: he played the piano and harmonica and encouraged others to express their singing talents. I sang and played the guitar with him and when he formed a musical group, I joined it. On Saturday nights, we made the rounds of local bars in downtown Snohomish.

Ted was so well liked that wherever we went people applauded and begged us to sing. Since I was the only Hispanic in the group, people asked me to sing Spanish songs. I have to say that I enjoyed this because even if I sometimes confused the lyrics and sang off key, it didn't matter to my audience. They were all of different nationalities and they didn't know the difference. With a few drinks under their belts, whatever I did sounded good to them. In every bar we went into, the patrons bought us drinks, so it wasn't long before we were as smiley as they were.

The dark side of Ted's empire, so to say, showed up pretty early for me because I've always been an intuitive person. Maybe that's how I survived as a kid. My father, more than anyone, tried to kill this part of my spirit – unknowingly, I believe – but my inner spirit wouldn't allow him to do this. I always knew things, or felt things I didn't completely understand. I believe my guardian angels were there with me fine-tuning my spiritual senses and always showing me the way.

One thing I noticed right off was that there were women around Ted, too many women, I thought. These females catered to his every need, and they expressed an exalted reverence for him. It looked like everyone trusted Ted to a degree that left me to wonder about my own suspicions of him. Some families trusted Ted with their children and let them sleep at his house overnight.

I didn't feel comfortable with that so I never allowed our children to be at Ted's home without Loretta and me being there as well. Sleep-overs were out of the question. My inner spirit kept telling me, *something's out of harmony in Ted's life.* But then I also asked myself — who am I to question this dynamic spiritual and business leader? Especially since we were new to the organization and hadn't been there as long as the others. What did I really know? What evidence did I really have for my mistrust?

Ted questioned my loyalty to him one day as we were driving to town. I was sitting in the back seat when Ted told me, "You know, Joseph, I am starting to feel that I can start trusting you." I didn't answer him, but my inner spirit answered, *I still don't trust you, Ted.* I couldn't put my finger on it, but my gut feelings seriously questioned Ted's motives in serving his religious followers. I'd had doubts about Ted from the minute we moved to Snohomish, but I kept them to myself and sometimes, as I've been saying, I doubted myself as well. I didn't feel this way when I first met him in Tucson; he seemed different then. Had his quick rise to success changed him? But not in such a way that other people could see? Or was it just me?

One day Loretta and I were in the back yard of our home with our children. Loretta was sitting on a lawn chair, while Michel, Annette and little Joseph, were playing around her. I was occupied raking leaves, but I was carrying a heavy heart. What could I do about the weird feelings I had? Who could I tell who would believe me? Who could I trust?

I had, in fact, shared my suspicions with other elders about Ted's being surrounded by women and small children all the time, but they chastised me for questioning him.

I pondered my feelings of distrust towards Ted as I continued raking leaves. Finally, I couldn't deny what my spirit was telling me. So I told Loretta, "This may sound crazy, but I suspect Ted is having sexual relationships with some of the women in the group but even worse — with the small children as well."

No sooner were the words out of my mouth than I began to regret saying them. What hurt me the most, and very deeply, was that even my Loretta didn't believe me. "Oh, Joseph," she said, "you're always thinking about sex!" Right then and there, I swallowed my words and didn't bring the subject up again. But from that moment on, I felt like an outsider on the inner circle of Eden Farms. It was a strange place to be: in, and at the same time, out.

Little by little though, certain things started happening that I think got some of the other men thinking. One night Debbie, the young daughter of Jerry and Roberta Curtis ran away from Eden Farms. She was only thirteen. Ted and several other "loyalists" drove around town late into the night, looking for little Debbie. I was also there, sitting in the back seat. No one knew why she'd run away, but I was sure that I did........ All the while, Ted knew.

While we went looking for Debbie, I tried to suggest to Ted where she might have gone. He told me to shut up.

Debbie was not found that night. She had hidden herself very well and no one could find her. She never came back to Eden Farms and after that, Ted ordered all the adults to keep a close watch over all the other young girls and boys that lived within the compound. Later it was discovered state officials had placed Debbie in a foster home. Although we didn't know it at the time, later it became clear that when Debbie ran away, she had gone to law enforcement authorities and reported the abuse Ted was subjecting her to.

Since we lived in our own house in town and away from the Eden Farms compound, we were not aware of all that took place with other families and their children who lived within the confines of the compound at Eden Farms.

Nothing happened in regard to Debbie reporting Ted to authorities for a number of weeks, then all hell broke loose, as I will explain in a moment.

As it was, life went on as usual with Eden Farms and Ellogos, but Debbie's disappearance stayed with me as proof of the suspicions I'd had all along about Ted. Something was very wrong and I knew it, if no one else did.

One Saturday afternoon, I was doing carpentry work on the building adjoining Ted's house within the compound, as were many other men and boys working on the farm, when an army of cars rushed into the property. I wondered how they got in because the main front gate was always locked to keep out anyone who was not a member of Eden Farms or Ellogos.

Black-suited men with guns were waving their badges as they jumped out of their cars. One of them shouted, "All right, everyone stand still, drop your tools, and hold your hands above your heads!"

We all stared in surprise as the grounds were overrun by the sheriff's posse, state police, city police and the FBI. They swarmed into all the buildings, opening filing cabinets, confiscating records, opening every door to every room, and I wondered what was next – jail?

Within Ted's home compound, there was another home where Jerry Schindler, a former Catholic priest and his wife, Kathy, also a former Catholic nun, lived. Years earlier, they'd lost faith in the Catholic Church and had joined Ted Renaldo's program. I remember being held outside by an FBI agent, while another agent banged on the door of the home where Jerry and Kathy lived. I could hear this agent shouting, "Ma'am, open the door, open your door right now." To which Kathy responded, "No I won't. Get away from my house, you are not going to come in."

After all these years, I am feeling very emotional as I share this story. My mind suddenly rushing me back to that day when so many police officers were running around the property looking for Ted. What was this all about? But I knew the answer.

In a little while, Ted Renaldo was led out of his house in hand cuffs, flanked by several police officers and FBI men.

That started a terrible commotion. Women, children and even men were screaming, crying and demanding for Ted's release. Seeing their spiritual leader hauled away to jail like a common criminal was too much for them.

It wasn't long before all the major newspapers, radio stations and TV stations were on top of this story. *The Everett Herald* of Everett, Washington was taking the lead in covering the story for Snohomish County.

The investigation lasted a full year. Then it was another year before Ted was brought to trial. Loretta and I attended one of the hearings where we observed Ted sitting with his attorney and Donna Peterson, his faithful puppet, sitting to his left and Cathy, his wife at his right hand. I don't know how Ted knew that Loretta and I were sitting about five rows behind him and to his left, but at one point, he turned around and made eye contact with me and maintained it as if trying to stare me down. I had a cold look in my eyes, I know, and we locked on each other for a short while.

The judge ordered Ted to be jailed for the entire time of his trial and imposed an extraordinarily high bail. One night I went to the jail, as much as anything, I wanted to know how Ted might've reacted to my interviews with the FBI. I didn't know if he hated me or had no feeling at all about me.

I went there to see his reaction to my presence; I was perhaps looking for some kind of closure. Ted didn't see me at first when he entered the small holding room where other prisoners were visiting with family, but at one point, I knew he'd become aware of me standing there looking at him. Suddenly, Donna and Cathy, who were there visiting Ted, turned around and stared at me and I saw a bewildered look which quickly changed to glaring anger. I knew at that moment that Ted felt uncomfortable and possibly threatened by my presence.

Ted positioned himself so that Donna and Cathy would hide him and keep me from making eye contact with him. I took a few steps in another direction so I could see him again, but always he shifted around out of sight. I finally walked up close to the visitors window to face him and gave him a smile, then I left the building. I never saw Ted again, except in the newspapers, and I have never heard from him since.

In the end, Ted was charged with the sexual abuse of several minors. Testimony in court by young girls told of how he would take showers with them, have sex with them, and in some cases, raped them.

The whole mess was infernally tragic and sad. Ted was sentenced to prison for ten years. The community of Snohomish was in shock.

Here was a man who was liked and respected as a successful businessman; a man who also served as the president of the Snohomish Chamber of Commerce; a man who had been campaign chairman for a candidate running for sheriff. Ted was well known in business circles comprised of high level business executives for large corporations.

To this day it saddens me to think that a person with such potential, especially in accomplishing phenomenal success in the world of business, could go so wrong in life. All the businesses he started, by the way, continued for a time, but the bad publicity of Ted's conviction took its toll and the businesses began to erode. In the end, almost all closed their doors or went bankrupt.

Many of the families involved with the group left. Ted's actions also brought about the divorce of several couples and the children who were victimized by Ted required a lot of professional counseling. All in all, it took about seven years before the members of Ted's cult realized that my earliest suspicions, which I'd shared with them, were founded on the truth.

I may have come out of this mess unscathed, but it was a great reminder to me to always trust my inner feelings, my instincts, my guardian angels, who, unlike me, have never doubted or deserted me. Quite often, we tend to doubt our spiritual powers. It is so easy to accord others the strength that we, in truth, have within ourselves.

Every one of us has spiritual strength and resilience and the ability to see what is on the road ahead. But we need to recognize this, and more importantly, to honor it, in order to treasure the blessing that is our birthright.

Life Changing Experiences

I have found that with every change in my life there are new and valuable lessons to be learned. The experiences in Snohomish certainly fall into this category.

New experiences are welcome to an open and receptive mind, but you have to recognize and embrace the lessons. There is wealth in letting go of hurtful feelings. Holding on to old grudges and resentments prevents positive blessings from manifesting, because when one is full of negativism, there's no room for the positive. When we unclutter our mind, our spirit is free to let fresh energy come into our lives.

While we remained in Snohomish, we continued to operate the floor covering business, all the while planning for a move back to Las Vegas, New Mexico. Our true friends in Snohomish tried to dissuade us from selling our business and moving away. One after another said — "You've worked so many years building up your business . . . and now you're just going to give it all up?"

It was 1979, five years after moving to Snohomish, when we finally sold our company and once again rented a large U-Haul trailer, loaded up our things and returned to the town where Loretta and I had begun our lives. We arrived in Las Vegas in time to enjoy Thanksgiving Day with Loretta's family.

We were happy to be back home with family. Loretta's father had passed away a few years earlier, my mother had been fighting cancer for about ten years, so some things had changed or were changing, but overall it was a good time, and our children really enjoyed being with their cousins.

After all I had been through and learned about life and love, I was looking forward to patching up things with my father. I felt it was important for my children to get to know him since he was their only living grandfather. Little did I know that my father was still holding on to his own demons of inner anger. I felt he blamed me and my family for many of his own problems and as a result of this, I was never really able to patch up much of anything with him. For some reason, he wouldn't, or couldn't, open up. I was thus unable to enter his world, which made it impossible to get to know the man. Sadly, he would forever remain a stranger to me, and my children never got to know him as a grandfather.

There are two sad memories regarding my father that my kids have mentioned at various times. One was the day he took a large paper sack, packed in it every family and kid's pictures I had sent to him over the years, went to our home on Williams Drive, and dumped them on my doorstep. The other was when we met him in a grocery store and my kids ran up to him yelling, "Grandpa, Grandpa —" as they grabbed his pant leg, but he simply shook them off his leg like they were annoying little animals. My children were very young at the time, but to this day, they still remember that. Sadly, my father never gave my children a chance to get to know him — or that part of him that was good. I think he took all his negative feelings he had towards me and transferred them to my children.

I had no time to dwell on past grudges as I got busy looking for a job. I went through a phase of discouragement for a while. I couldn't find a job, my family and I were living with my mother-in-law and my kids were sleeping on sleeping bags on the floor. Sometimes I wondered if I'd done the right thing by selling my business and coming home to more headaches and woes.

But I held on to my desire of wanting to find a good job that would get me back into circulation in the community. As it happened I met Carlos Lopez and Chris Gallegos who owned KNMX radio, and they hired me part time. Mr. Lopez told me I had a good voice for radio and I spoke Spanish. I trained under him for a week, *without pay*, after which he assigned me to the morning wake up show, gave me keys for the front door and turned me loose, mistakes and all. I loved radio and I learned the ropes fast, especially because it was a Spanish music format.

I was with this job for about eight months when I got a call from my brother Fred and he told me that Mr. Dennis Mitchell, the manager of KFUN radio was in need of a full time Spanish program director and Spanish announcer.

This is my brother Fred working at KABQ radio in Albuquerque, New Mexico

Fred by the way also started in radio broadcasting at KFUN in the mid 70's and went on to become one of the top Spanish radio and TV Spanish news anchors in Albuquerque for KLUZ Channel 41, *where he was regarded as, the voice of New Mexico*. He was my hero and mentor when it came to broadcasting. Actually, Fred has always been my mentor since we were small kids.

In 1980, I visited Dennis Mitchell at KFUN and applied for the full time position as Spanish Program Director and Spanish radio announcer. I got the job and I was excited about working at the original, *heritage* radio station in Las Vegas.

Meanwhile, Loretta had grown tired of her job and was looking for something else. As it turned out, Dennis had a job opening for a receptionist and traffic controller. He hired Loretta for the job. That's how we both started working at KFUN and KLVF radio. The years passed and we both enjoyed our jobs. I loved the music and also was happy that working at the radio station offered me the opportunity to get back into circulation with the community. This had been a goal of mine since living in Snohomish. I used to tell Loretta that when we moved back to Las Vegas, I wanted to get into a job that would quickly get me back into circulation in the community and introduced to the movers and shakers in the business circles, and now it was coming to pass through radio.

Working in radio, one never knows who will walk in through the front door. I have met and interviewed many elected officials, including local, state and federal politicians, many New Mexico Governors, and several popular music artists and movie stars.

I was kept very busy selling advertising, doing production of commercials, collections and customer relations along with being on the air during my Spanish program four hours a day Monday through Friday and often on weekends.

Loretta was also discovering her broadcasting abilities. After finishing her regular duties at the end of the day, she would host her own country show from five to seven Monday through Friday evenings. Our three kids would come to the station after school and be with us, so little by little, they started getting interested in radio. In time, during their middle and high school years, they worked nights and weekends. I remember Joseph Jr. would sit on Loretta's lap as she was hosting her show. She let him handle the controls so that by the time he was eight years old, he could do it all by himself.

Through my radio work I was elected to city council where I served for twelve consecutive years. I loved public service, but absolutely hated the politics. Especially dirty politics. Some people might say, is there any other kind?

Working in radio and serving as a city councilman was a good fit. Via the airwaves, I was able to keep the community informed about city matters and decisions made during council meetings. Some of my fellow councilmen and the mayor at the time did not always agree with me doing this. By the way, its interesting how circles come around. I served under the administrations of two different mayors. One mayor was my long time childhood friend........Tony Martinez.

Two major projects I took a major role in accomplishing were traveling to Washington, D. C. on two separate occasions to lobby for funding to build a railroad overpass off University Avenue in Las Vegas. When I was first elected, I became aware of the need for such an overpass. There were hundreds of residents whose homes got locked in between the railroad tracks and I-25 when the freeway was built. When a train came into the city and stopped at the depot, it would block all five railroad crossings so that emergency vehicles couldn't cross the tracks to assist those in need. Residents asked me to correct this dangerous problem. Because emergency crews could not cross the tracks blocked by trains, certain people had died from heart attacks, others had lost homes to fire and injured children were prevented from getting to the hospital. I was totally shocked to find out that this was happening to these residents. So, in 1988, Las Vegas city manager Les Montoya along with several other councilors and I traveled to Washington to meet with our Washington representatives to inform them about this issue. Then Mr. Montoya and I returned to Washington to assist then Congressman Bill Richardson in our efforts to obtain federal funding. While there, we lobbied to obtain four million dollars to help build the railroad overpass. Congressman Bill Richardson lobbied with us and presented the issue to the appropriations committee. Congressman Pete Domenici, and Senator Jeff Bingaman supported our funding request as well when it came to a vote. Bill Richardson went on to serve as U. S. Ambassador under President Clinton, he also served as governor of New Mexico and was a candidate in the race for president as well.

In preparing for our trip to Washington, Congressman Richardson instructed us to prepare a manuscript outlining the issue in clear, concise detail but no longer than three minutes. All the city staff that developed the manuscript did a wonderful and professional job in preparing the document. When it came time for Les and me to present our funding request before the appropriations committee, Richardson kept motioning to me with his hands to be sure to keep my presentation to three minutes. I assured him that I had memorized every word and I would keep it to three minutes.

At the same hearing, there was a large group from California who were also lobbying the appropriations committee for money and who were scheduled to speak ahead of us. This worried me because this group went on and on for half an hour because several people addressed the committee. I could see the frustration in the eyes of the chairman and many committee members because this California group was taking up too much of the committee's time. I mentioned to Les that when it came to us, the committee was going to be too upset and maybe deny our request.

Left to right. This is a photo of Councilman Joseph P. Baca, U. S. Congressman Bill Richardson and Les Montoya, Las Vegas city manager, lobbying in Washington, D. C. for federal funding to build the Railroad overpass.

By the way. Les was not asleep during my presentation. He was deep in meditation praying for the funding.

Mean while, Richardson kept looking my way with three fingers raised and a stern look on his face. I knew what that look meant. *Keep it to three minutes Joseph.* The California group finally finished with their presentation and as they walked away from the table, the chairman of the appropriations committee stopped them dead in their tracks and said, *hold it, a word of advice for the California group. Next time you come before this or any other committee in Washington asking for money, remember this, less is always better.* At that moment, I realized Richardson's wisdom and insight in instructing me to, *keep it to three minutes.* I did and as we rose from our chairs, I thanked them for their time and consideration and we walked away. Three weeks later, Congressman Richardson called the city to say the committee approved our funding request and our bill was on President Clinton's desk for signing. We got the four million dollars to build the Railroad Over Pass.

At the state level, Senators Alfred Nelson, and Joe Page, *now deceased* and Representatives Sam Vigil helped obtain funding from the state for the building of the Railroad Overpass. Today, that overpass is constructed just a short distance away from KFUN and I pass by it every day on my way to work.

I also organized a trip to Camp McGregor in Texas to visit National Guard members of the 720th unit before they were deployed to Iraq for Desert Storm. When word got out that I would be visiting the troops, families delivered hundreds of packages of frozen chili, tortillas, assorted gifts, and other dried foods to my home so that we could deliver these items to their loved ones. Many of my friends were in this unit and I could see tears streaming down their faces when I handed them their packages. I also walked from one fox hole to another with my recording equipment. I taped Christmas greetings from the service men and women to their families. Arnold Trujillo, a videographer with Luna Community College followed me with his camera filming a movie that was aired over cable TV during the holidays. The Holiday greetings were aired over KFUN and KLVF during the Christmas and New Year holiday. A reporter from the *Las Vegas Optic* and one from the *Albuquerque Journal* also made the trip and wrote wonderful photographically illustrated stories about the 720th and their mission. Les Montoya also made the trip while Col. Zek Ortiz arranged for full government clearance for every member of our group.

In 1992, another change took place in my life. I think I had gotten burned out working in radio, so I left KFUN. I was experiencing some frustration with my job because I didn't have any say so in the decision making process of the business and I saw so much untapped and undeveloped potential at the stations and felt limited in what I could accomplish. Meanwhile, Loretta stayed on and continued working for Mr. Mitchell for about three months. I started working as the manager of Colortime, a furniture rental business and I hired Loretta to work with me. So, for now, both Loretta and I were out of radio broadcasting.

I was gone from radio for about six years and I missed it tremendously and felt totally lost and out of touch with the community. I missed keeping informed about local and national news. I felt as if the world was passing me by. During my absence form radio, I worked at different jobs including the *Las Vegas Optic* in advertising sales. For a period of about three months, both Loretta and I actually managed KNMX radio while the two owners were contesting ownership in court. We thought of buying KNMX but that was not to be.

As in the past, my spirit was speaking to me again. All during the time I was gone from radio, I told Loretta that I knew someday I would return to KFUN. I didn't know how, or when, but I knew I would be back.

Sure enough, while I was working part time at the *Optic*, and another job, I would frequently visit Dennis Mitchell at KFUN. One day I bravely asked if he would sell me the stations. Dennis told me he needed my help covering the Spanish program because his DJ would be absent for a few weeks. While I was hosting the Spanish program, he fired his morning DJ, and that's when Dennis asked me to come back to work for him full time. I did.

The stage was quietly being set for my longtime relationship with KFUN and KLVF radio. I believe my hovering angels were already working in the unseen spirit world arranging for my long time union with the love of my life, KFUN and KLVF, as will be seen shortly. Something was soon to happen that would change my life forever.

My Return to Radio

My leave of absence from KFUN and KLVF was actually a good thing for me. Being away from it helped me realize how much I really loved broadcasting. I could also see how radio communicated on a broad scale, affecting people's lives. It had certainly influenced my life in a positive way, so when I returned to broadcasting, I brought a new dedication and commitment to serve the community. With renewed energy and focus, I started to generate greater income for the stations. Maybe I didn't know it fully at the time, but, in reality, my family and I were being groomed as the future owners of the stations. Once again though, I'm getting ahead of myself.

The hardest part of my job was, and still is, getting up at 3:30 each morning to be at work by 4:30. I am often asked how I do it to get up so early and yet work up to 14 or 15 hours a day including many weekends. My answer is simply that I love my job, and radio to me is not really work. To be successful at what you do, you have to love your work. I wake up mornings with a quiet prayer thanking God for permitting me to have such a unique opportunity of working with my family and to serve others.

Now and then, I realize how many people hate the work they do. They loathe getting up in the morning, commuting in traffic, and finally reporting to a job that involves no hope of advancement plus a day full of delirium detail and often back-stabbing politics. Many people I've talked to have gotten physically ill from the very thing that should be sustaining and inspiring them. Therefore their work is their nemesis. They can see no end to their labor and yet no future in terms of what they want to do. Worse still — many people have no idea what their ideal job might be.

Well, now that I was back in radio broadcasting, doing what I loved best, I continued to dream of ownership. More than anything, I wanted to be the owner-manager of the two stations I now worked for.

Now for more than twenty years I'd faithfully practiced a simple ritual. Call it dreaming if you will, or perhaps wishing, but I call it silent prayer.

Nonetheless, a simple daily ritual, but it was more than that, too. Sometimes my burning desire consumed me. Sometimes it brought me to tears.

Arriving at work at 4:30 a. m., I unlocked the front gate and proclaimed in an audible voice, "Good morning, KFUN and KLVF hill, I love you, and one of these days I am going to own you and you are going to be mine."

I'd repeat this refrain as I drove up the dark winding dirt road to the front parking lot. Then, unlocking the front door of the building, I'd say my shorter but no less heartfelt version – "Good morning, KFUN and KLVF. I love you and one day I am going to own you and you will be mine."

My words were filled with faith and belief in myself.

By speaking out in this way, I dedicated myself to my dream.

At home, I constantly spoke to Loretta about my dream, so much so, that I think I wore her out with my obsession. But who else could I share my dream with? She was the only one and she supported me.

Then, one day in 2004, my dream evaporated into thin air. The station owner, Dennis Mitchell informed me that he'd just sold the stations; had in fact signed a contract agreement with Will Sims and his partner Don Davis. Both men were long time broadcasters and owners of other stations.

My heart sank when I heard the news.

Following this, I sat at my desk in a dark mood that, moment by moment, was getting worse. I called Loretta to tell her the bad news – "Loretta, my dream of owning the stations is gone! Dennis just sold them to someone else." As I said this, my voice, usually strong and firm, sounded quavery.

"No honey," she said, "don't give up. Anything can happen. What are you going to do - - close the door on your dream? You have been feeding this dream for over twenty years, you can't give up now." In my heart I knew Loretta was right and her words rekindled my desire to buy the stations.

I congratulated Dennis on his business deal, and then I sat at my computer and up-dated my resume. I knew I would most likely need to re-apply for my job with the new owners. To my surprise, Mr. Sims immediately asked me to be manager of both stations. Naturally, I accepted.

On June 4, 2004, Will Sims, Dennis Mitchell and I sat at Charlie's Spic-N- Span restaurant having lunch as both men signed the final paper work. Will handed Dennis a fat check, and the deal was sealed. Actually, I felt happy for both men because Dennis had told me previously that he was ready to get out of the broadcasting business and retire. Will Sims now had what he wanted, the radio stations *KFUN/AM* and *KLVF/FM*. As for me, I was happy and grateful to have a job.

I accepted the fact that the stations now had new owners and they were my new bosses. My responsibility was to do my best in managing the stations and there was a lot of work ahead of me. I had no staff, except a Spanish DJ who didn't like me because he knew I was going to make some changes. He was right in thinking this: the guy had an attitude, not to mention poor work habits. It wasn't long before Mr. Sims told me that this same guy was calling him at night and saying he couldn't work for me. "I just told him you were my business manager, and that you were also in charge of operations," Will said.

Well, the guy had no plans of resigning or quitting, he was simply trying to create problems for me. When he didn't make it to work for several days, I had to let him go.

So now I had no staff. Just a young girl, an intern that I'd accepted through a local social program.

Here is how my typical day went. At work by 3:30 a. m., hosting the morning wake up show starting at 6 a. m. and the talk show "Over The Back Fence" which ended at 10. Then for the rest of the morning I did sales, recorded new commercials, did collections, broadcast the news, then at 1: p. m., I was the Spanish program announcer on the Spanish program which ended at 4:30 p. m., when I was finally off the air. After that, I had the rest of the afternoon to finish my computer business. After closing the station, I arrived home at 6:30, too tired to eat dinner. I took a shower and went right to sleep.

But, then my lifesaver/partner came to my rescue, as always. Loretta told Mr. Sims I was working too hard and very long hours and that if I got ill, I'd be of no use to him or to her. "Why don't you hire me to help my husband?" Loretta asked. "You can pay me what I am earning at my current job, and I'll come to work for you right away." Mr. Sims came directly to me and said, "Hire Loretta." So I did and just like that, there we were, working together again. We've always worked as a team and I was so relieved to have her on board. However, in reality, we now worked long hours together.

Then another blessing . . . Joseph Jr. our son JR, as he likes to be called, came to Mr. Sims and said he'd like to work for the station, too. He said to

Mr. Sims, if he paid him what he was earning at his current job, he would come right to work. Mr. Sims called me into his office and said, "Joseph, hire JR." So I did. My plan was falling into place. And what a blessing to have my family with me all of the time.

I have to say though, looking back, I can see the wisdom of the universe at work. I still didn't know how or when it would happen, but my faith was strong and I still said my daily prayer of ownership and believed that one day . . . my dream would come true.

Then one day I got a call from Mr. Sims. I was not aware that he was building another radio station in Santa Fe and only had months in which to get it on the air as per FCC regulations.

"Joseph," he began, "I'm building a station in Santa Fe. I can't be in two places at once, so I need to sell one of the stations. You know, I was looking at your resume and realized you'd be the perfect person to own KFUN. You've been working there for a very long time, you're from Las Vegas, everyone in the community knows and respects you. So, are you interested?"

"Yes," I said. "But it depends on your asking price and terms and most importantly, if I can get the funding."

Bravely spoken but – how to get the funding? Loretta and I had been pondering this seriously since 2000. Would the local banks support us? In October of that year, we were having lunch at the Ore House Restaurant in Santa Fe. We were sitting at our table deep in thought and discussion over a cold beer, as to how we were going to come up with the money to purchase KFUN radio. I had noticed a man sitting on a corner table in the restaurant writing or scribbling on a paper but gave it little thought. Then the man approached our table, "excuse me he said, then handed me a folded napkin and walked away. I unfolded the napkin and immediately was overcome with emotion. The man was a sketch artist and had sketched a drawing of Loretta and I deep in thought as we sat at our table.

I bought the man a beer and walked to his table to thank him. "Sir, thank you very much for this drawing of my wife and me. You have no idea what this means to us". Well he said, "you two looked so seriously deep in thought and you stood out from all the crowd, that I felt compelled to draw you". This sketch now sits in a frame at KFUN with a picture of KFUN hill and the building and serves as another daily reminder of how blessed we are.

This is an artist pencil sketch drawing of Loretta and me inside the Ore
House Restaurant in Santa, Fe, New Mexico, deep in thought about how
we were going to buy KFUN and KLVF radio.

For the next eight months we worked on a business plan. Thanks to the
valuable help from Don Bustos and his staff at the Small Business Development
Center at Luna Community College, we developed a workable plan that I hand-
delivered to all three local banks in town. Then Loretta and I waited for their
reply. We felt fairly confident all three banks would help but as it turned out, one
bank turned us down, another bank never got back to us, and then we started to
wonder if we'd get funded at all. Maybe it was all an impossible dream. Well, I
chased away that thought pretty quickly.

Then our prayers were answered. Community 1st Bank, (then First National
Bank), called and said they wanted to meet with us to discuss our business plan.
They agreed to support our dream and to fund our purchase of KFUN, the
building, the tower, all the equipment and four acres of land. They were ready
to lend us $450,000. We had plenty of collateral with our home, cars and

property, and of course KFUN and all that came with it. But we needed hard cash as a down payment.

Now, we wondered, where would we find $100,000 for the down payment? As it was, Loretta and I had already used our personal credit card to pay $10,000 in legal fees to our attorney in Washington. This by the way, was money we would never get back and could not claim on our taxes as a business expense because we paid these expenses before we owned KFUN. But, we were determined to accomplish our dream.

At the bank's request, Mr. Mitchell agreed leave $100,000 from his sale of the stations in the bank as cash collateral so that we could qualify for the bank loan. We will always be grateful to the Mitchells for their help. Meanwhile, the rest of Dennis's full payoff for the stations wouldn't be realized until KLVF was sold.

So, in February of 2006 we became the proud owners of radio station KFUN, the original heritage station of Las Vegas, New Mexico, our home town. We felt so thankful to Community 1st Bank for supporting our dream.

The reverse side of this post card reads the following:
Ruts of the original Santa Fe Trail can still be seen on station property.
The main structure is adobe. Elevation 6,550 feet. The Pecos Arroyo skirts the bluff.
First broadcast Christmas Day 1941. Founded by Dorothy and Ernie Thwaites.

After purchasing KFUN, we had to buckle down and sell lots of advertising to cover our mortgage and pay all monthly expenses. But we were ecstatic, to say the least. We'd achieved one half of our goal. Now, to fulfill the whole thing, we needed to buy the FM station KLVF.

But, how in the world were we going to come up with $650,000?

Little did we know that there was another blessing coming our way.

Please turn the page for the rest of that story, and share in the most amazing blessing of all!

You'll Never Accomplish Anything In Your Life

Many of my childhood friends could not believe that I, the kid from our poor neighborhood now was the proud owner of the radio station they grew up listening to, KFUN/AM 1230. *La Voz del pueblo. The voice of the meadow city.*

How do you think I felt, when my father's words still rang out loud and clear in my mind.

You'll never be worth a damn.

You'll never accomplish anything in your life.

Was there something wrong with this picture? Here I was, the owner of the sixth oldest radio station in New Mexico and the original heritage radio station in our community, yet, I wasn't worth a damn?

Sadly for me, I would never get the chance to share my joy with my dear father. He passed away on November 03, 2000.

How I yearn for my father to be with me today so I could pick him up in the morning, go for breakfast or just a hot cup of coffee, and then bring him to *my radio stations* so he could spend the day with me.

KFUN was now under the ownership of *Baca Broadcasting LLC.* Our team including Loretta and me as 50/50 partners and our son Joseph Jr. We had a few temporary employees, but it was always a struggle keeping a Spanish program announcer. They either quit on me or wanted to do their own thing and I would end up firing them. When that happened, I was faced with hosting the Spanish program along with my morning wake up show, the talk show and many other duties. Loretta and I always wanted to bring our older son Michel and our daughter Annette into the business. Both had full time jobs, but I told Michel I was hiring him as the weekday Spanish announcer. Annette wanted to keep her job at Community 1st Bank, so we brought Michel into the business. He was such a charm. Good at his job and responsible for remodeling the entire building. Both our sons excelled in their jobs.

Shown in this photo are: In back ground, Michel, me in the middle, and J. R in the forefront.

Every day I thank God, that now I have both my sons working with me and have the opportunity to build a strong father and son relationship with them. This is another blessing in my life and an opportunity I never had with my father. As a family, we all kept very busy managing KFUN. But Loretta and I were now contemplating as to how we were going to get the funding to buy KLVF/FM radio. We needed and wanted the FM station to supplement our income and to better serve our community and increase our audience.

Once again we turned to Mr. Don Bustos and his very capable staff to assist us in developing a business plan. I was a little better at doing this the second time around because I had gone through this process in preparing to purchase KFUN. As it turned out, there was no need for us to submit a business plan. As you read on, you will see what I mean.

Meanwhile, we started meeting with our bankers at Community 1st Bank where Mr. Ernesto Salazar again gave his 100% support and effort in working out a funding plan to present to the bank board. We thank both Mr. Keith Tucker, bank president and Ernesto for their dedication and assistance and supporting our long range business plans, including the bank board members.

After many meetings, the bank assured us that they would fund our purchase of KLFV/FM.

One day, while hosting our talk show, Mrs. Joyce Litherland called me and assured me that they would support Loretta and me in any development we planned to do on KFUN hill. Ray and Joyce are the owners of Community 1st Bank. Her father, Mr. Ivan Hilton, a pillar of a man in our community, established the bank as, The First National Bank in 1949. We are thankful to Ray and Joyce Litherland for their support.

We were so happy that our bank once again was supporting our efforts. The plan was that they would finance us with 1.2 million with which to pay off the first mortgage when we purchased KFUN and all that came with it and the rest would go to purchasing KLVF.

WOW, we thought. 1.2 million. How would we ever pay that back? Surely not in our life time. I told our sons they would have to assume this mortgage in the end because Loretta and I would not live long enough to pay it off. But, we were fully committed to our goal and we were ready to assume the mortgage.

We once again hired our Washington attorney to start drawing up all the required paper work to be submitted to the FCC. We didn't anticipate any problems with the FCC approving our license application. But then our attorney, Peter Gutman from Washington, D. C. dropped a bomb on us. He informed us that in his research, he found documentation stating that in the year 2000, Mr. Mitchell had submitted an application with the FCC to have KLVF radio moved to Santa Fe making that it's city of license, and the application had been approved and accepted by the FCC. That meant that in a few years, KLVF would be moved out of Las Vegas and become a Santa Fe station.

This was very upsetting and I immediately contacted Will and Don and advised them that I was prepared to buy KLVF, but only as a Las Vegas station, not as a Santa Fe station. I told them they and their attorney had to petition the FCC to annul their decision and to re-assign the station license back to Las Vegas.

We soon became aware that we were in for a long and tough battle with the FCC. For the next year and a half, proposal after proposal went back and forth between my attorney and their attorney, with many changes made in each and every document. It got so hectic and frustrating because Will's attorney kept questioning whether I would be able to come up with the required funding which was over a half million dollars. I kept assuring them that my bank was committed to us and that the sale would be a cash deal. I received numerous email messages from my attorney and from the seller's attorney with many "what ifs" and many changes to the purchase agreement and the many legal documents. Mr. Salazar, our banker, even wrote a letter to all parties involved, assuring them that the bank guaranteed our financing and that they were committed to the Baca's. Even this didn't seem to matter to the sellers' attorneys. Our attorney's fees just kept increasing and increasing and my patience were growing thin and I finally got so fed up that I told the sellers and their attorney not to bother me anymore because I was no longer interested in buying their station.

Don't call me. I'll call you.

I guess this got their attention because soon after, I got an email from Mr. Sims apologizing that it was taking so long to consummate the deal and for the enormous attorney fees it was costing me. So, he offered to pay $5,000 toward my attorney fees if this would end up being a cash sale. The FCC was refusing to reverse their decision and insisted that KLVF was now assigned to Santa Fe and would be moved there soon and both attorneys were having zero success in getting the FCC to change their mind. They would not even consider the idea.

One day, I got an email from Will telling me that all efforts by the attorneys had failed and we were just going to have to fly to Washington to lobby the FCC and he asked if I would go with him.

"Of course" I said. "I'll go with you."

I prepared a one page document that outlined my appeal and prepared to present it to the FCC officials. I also wrote a letter to Mr. Rudy Bonacci, assistant chief with the FCC audio division, thanking him for agreeing to meet with us.

Our meeting got pretty heated between Will and the FCC officials. I just sat back and kept my cool. Then one of the gentleman said, "We already decided this issue and we are not changing anything. First you applied to move the station to Santa Fe, and now you are coming back asking us to reverse our decision. That is not going to happen."

Will assured them that it was not us that asked for the station to be moved to Santa Fe, but Mr. Mitchell. This was my understanding.

So then Will said, "Mr. Chairman, Mr. Baca came all the way from Las Vegas to state his case, would you be willing to listen to him?"

At this point, the chairman crossed his arms, turned his chair facing me, looked directly into my eyes and said, "Mr. Baca, this issue is not about Joseph

Baca, it's about which city is going to be better served by KLVF, and we believe that city is Santa Fe. But, go ahead and state your case, but at this point, you may just as well tell me about the weather in Las Vegas."

I took his cue when he said this issue was not about Joseph Baca. I used this to my advantage. "I fully agree with you Mr. Chairman, this issue is not at all about me, but about which community will be better served. That is exactly why I come before you today. Thank you for allowing me to present my views."

There was a very calm conversation between us – no tension or friction. He listened to my presentation and then quietly closed a file placed in front of him. I took this as a signal to stop talking and I simply relaxed into my chair.

Then the chairman said, "Look, we want to work with you. If you can prove to me why we should move KLVF back to Las Vegas and that the audience would increase, I will consider your appeal."

When I told him that we were located right off I-25, he then said, "Oh, that means travelers on I-25 are additional listeners and you play an important role in bringing visitors into the community." After much discussion, he then gave us thirty days to submit additional documents, at which time he would make his decision.

As the chairman and I walked down the hallway to his office, he told me that he was real good friends with a man from Las Vegas, another Baca, and wanted to know if I was related to him. I felt he was really wanting to connect with me. One thing though that really upset the chairman, was that we had contacted our elected representatives from New Mexico and asked for their assistance. Three times the chairman pointed at Will and said, "You called your representatives in Washington, you didn't have to call your senators. Don't call them again. They do sign our checks, but don't call them again." I thanked the chairman again and asked that he please take the time to read my letter I had left with him. He assured me he would read my letter. We shook hands and departed.

We flew back home and waited. Then sometime in May, I got a call from our attorney telling us the FCC had approved our application to reassign the license for KLVF back to Las Vegas. We had accomplished our goal.

Now we were ready to finalize our business deal. So we thought.

It took a year and a half and $35,000 in legal fees to settle this matter. I couldn't believe Loretta and I had dished out $35,000 in attorney's fees. This was money we desperately needed to apply towards our purchase, or new equipment, or to cover operational expenses. But I didn't want to dwell on this in a negative way. We counted our blessings and moved on. We were so excited to keep KLVF in the community.

Thank you God for our blessings. We still wondered though, how are we going to pay back $1.2 million dollars? We really needed a miracle.

This is a photo of our guest studio.

It's Only The Beginning

We succeeded in convincing the FCC to re-license KLVF radio to Las Vegas. Now what? We still didn't have the money to purchase it. Fortunately, our bank was still committed to lending us a business loan in the amount of $1.2 million. Loretta and I reviewed our business plan and sales projections to make sure we could handle our new mortgage of about $8,000 per month.

It was important that we reduce our overhead as well. We examined our P&L report, checking each line item and eliminating as many of our monthly expenses as possible. The end result was that we reduced our expenses by $15,000. This would surely please our bank and look good on our loan application.

We met often with our banker, Mr. Salazar who worked with us in planning our financing. I have to admit, I was scared to assume a loan for $1.2 million dollars. But Loretta and I felt we had no other choice if we wanted to own KLVF radio. I don't like to second guess my decisions, but I also don't believe in jumping blindly into a business venture. If there was ever a time that we needed a blessing, it was now.

So now we were looking at getting in debt for way over a million.

Yet there was no way around it.

Time passed, we continued to do our job of managing KFUN and I faithfully continued to say prayers of thanks for the many blessings I'd already received. I also re-affirmed my determination to own KLVF and all the property on KFUN hill.

I especially had my eye set on the land that sits on the Southwest corner facing I-25 and the community. I kept telling Loretta that I goofed when negotiating the property boundaries of the land we'd purchased with KFUN. I told her I needed the Southwest corner because that is where I believed we should put up a new building for both stations.

I don't believe in luck. I believe that in life, we attract what we desire, and what we work for. We blaze our own trail. We choose our own direction in life. We control our own destiny. We decide how to live our lives and we determine if our every day will be positive and productive.

I believe if you get up with a negative attitude, you'll have that kind of day. The choice is ours to do with as you will. Therefore it's important to make the right choice.

So we continued working with our banker to fine tune the loan application. One thing kept coming up – the asking price for KLVF, $600,000. Several times I emailed Will and told him that the price was too high. And he'd write back, "*Joseph the asking price is what it is because that's what the station is worth.*"

I responded by saying that when I bought KFUN, at least I got a building, the tower, lots of equipment and four acres of land and the license. With my purchase of KLVF, I am not getting any of that. Besides this is a cash sale.

We were so close to finalizing the deal and I think my questions must have gotten Will thinking. A later email said: "*Joseph, KLVF is worth every bit of the asking price, but I will gladly throw in the land with the business deal.*"

This took us by surprise (even our banker) because Will had been advertising the land for a few years but no buyer had come forth. I quickly accepted his offer and now all I needed was to have our application approved by the bank board. Meanwhile, our attorney in Washington was still on the clock at $300 an hour and he'd stay on that clock until the closing of the sale.

Another big blessing was about to come our way.

One thing I have always done, is to buy lottery tickets. I buy them every Wednesday and every Saturday. For years I'd been telling Loretta, "Just watch, babe, one day I'm going to win a million dollars." She had her doubts, but in any case I believed it when I said it..

Actually, I'd never won much of anything – 7 dollars here, 12 dollars there, and one time I won twenty bucks.

I normally bought my tickets at different outlets. But my most convenient place was at Ross Gas Station on the corner of Grand Avenue and University, right down the street from KFUN. I usually bought about 6 dollars worth of tickets, but I always bought a power ball lottery ticket with the power play. That's a ticket where you pay the extra dollar for a chance to double your winnings, if you win. Normally I buy my tickets, put them in my pocket and forget about them for a few days, usually until the day when the lottery drawing is held.

On this particular day, which happened to be a Tuesday, I went to Better Stop, a convenience store owned by the Franken family on North Grand Avenue to fill up my car with gas. That night, I was taking my family to a concert in Santa Fe to see the Gipsy Kings. While signing my ticket for the gas I'd just purchased, I asked the clerk to check my lottery tickets. Then, I heard the machine sing, followed by a gasp from the clerk and her quietly saying, "You're a lucky guy."

"What did you say?"

Another clerk came forward. "What's going on?" The first clerk said, "Check this out . . . Oh my God!"

"No way!" said the second clerk. She looked at me and added in astonishment — "You just won a million dollars!!!" Then she held the receipt up to my face. I got it and started to walk out. As I approached the door, the clerk shouted, "Wait! Who are you?"

"I'm Joseph Baca, the owner of KFUN radio."

From my cell phone, I called Loretta at the station. "Babe! Guess what? I just won one million dollars with a $2.00 lottery power ball ticket!

There was a long silence. . . . .

Finally, she said, "Yah, right."

"Loretta, I'm not kidding."

"Well,. . . . . you're always joking about winning a million dollars."

"Loretta, who's joking? I've always told you that one day I would win a million bucks."

I rushed back to the station and even while holding my lottery receipt, Loretta still didn't believe me, neither did Joseph, our son. I went into my office, called the lottery headquarters in Albuquerque. "Sir, can you tell me what the tax amount would be if someone won a million dollars?

"Well . . . I'm not exactly sure. Maybe about $300, 000. Why do you ask? Is this a rhetorical question, or did you . . . ."

"I did,". . . . . I answered.

"Remember, be sure and sign the back of your ticket right away sir."

That's when I realized I didn't have my winning ticket with me.

In my excitement, I'd walked out of the store with nothing but a lottery receipt, and the wrong one at that.

I rushed back to the store and the moment I walked in the door, the clerk said, "Sir, I have your ticket and your receipt right here."

The first clerk must have been more shocked than I because she had even given me the store's receipt instead of mine.

Can you imagine, I had left my *unsigned winning lottery ticket with the clerk!*

Lucky for me, all the clerks were honest people.

A $2.00 lottery ticket and the little boy from the poor side of town, who'd always been told he wasn't worth anything had just become a millionaire. And after so many years of telling my wife this was going to happen, she finally believed me.

We went to meet with our banker, Ernesto Salazar at Community 1ˢᵗ Bank, and I told him I would no longer need to borrow his 1.2 million dollars to buy KLVF, he said, "What's wrong Joseph, did the deal fall through? What's going on?"

"No Ernesto, nothing's wrong. I don't need to borrow your money anymore because I just won a million dollar lottery jackpot."

"No way, get outta here, no way, get out!"

I looked at him calmly. "Yes Ernesto, it's true. Now I would like to deposit my winnings in your bank as soon as possible."

Loretta and me holding our BIG $1,000,000 lottery check

A few days passed, when I got an email from Will who now lived in Puerto Rico, *Congratulations Joseph, I hear you're now a millionaire.*

"*Yes, Will,*" I wrote back, "*Didn't I tell you all along that my purchase of KLVF was going to be a cash deal?*"

By the way, Will did pay $5,000 toward my legal fees, which he had promised to do if my purchase of KLVF was a cash deal.

So, my long time visualization (over twenty years of effort) to own both KFUN and KLVF radio and all the property on KFUN hill, had finally come to pass.

Amazed, my wife Loretta said, "Joseph, you finally got everything you always said you wanted."

I said, "Of course, Loretta. I got it because that's *exactly* what I always wanted." I had actually acquired KLVF and all the land on the hill for the price of a $2.00 lottery ticket.

What I always say is — If you're going to dream, dream big!

Loretta, my anchor and strength at KFUN & KLVF.

Michel, the roadrunner . Our eldest son, host of the Spanish program on KFUN/AM

Joseph. (J. R. Baca) our youngest son host of the oldies program on KLVF/FM

This is our lovely, free spirit daughter Annette.

Alicia Baca our granddaughter

Jerry Baca our grandson.

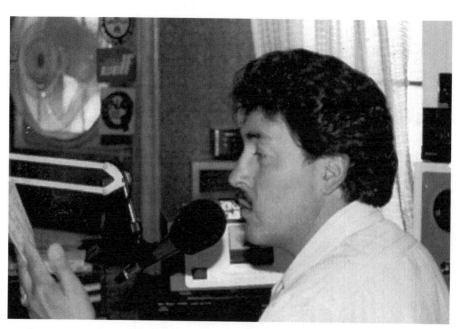

J. P. Baca at work, doing what he loves best.

Blessings In Disguise

Some people say that mishaps and mistakes, and even minor missteps arrive in our lives as curses. Some go so far as to say these things come as a punishment from God. Yet others insist that life is only a matter of good and bad luck, the spin of a wheel, the arc of heavenly bodies that determine our worth astrologically, our good or ill-fortune according to the stars of destiny. But as I believe I have demonstrated in my life story, the things that have happened to me have mostly been little *milagros*. The worst tragedies have over time assumed a different reality for me. Tragic events later morphed into that old expression "blessings in disguise." This is especially true if we accept them as such. And, as you know, I do.

Allow me to explain.

My biggest gift – winning the $1,000,000 lottery on August 9, 2008 – was closely followed by a blessing of another kind: losing the vision in my right eye. By the way, did I mention that I won the lottery on my mother's date of birth? Yes, August 9th.

It was early Friday on September 18th as I went for a walk on KFUN hill. The minute I stepped outside, I started sneezing, coughing and I had a runny nose. I completed my walk, wondering if I was getting sick. I didn't feel sick. But returning to my work, I continued to have watery eyes. Later that day, I visited our family doctor who confirmed I was suffering from a spate of allergies.

Although I went about my business for the rest of that week, my eyes still did not feel quite right and in addition my vision seemed somewhat blurred. Since I was still having eye trouble, I visited another doctor, one who lives next door to us. Our neighbor and friend, Bob. Unfortunately, he wasn't at home.

Later in the day, I was watching TV. For some reason, I covered my right eye to see what would happen. I could see fine. I then covered my left eye and immediately called out to Loretta, who was in the kitchen: "Loretta, I can't see out of my right eye."

Our daughter, Annette, ran to the neighbor doctor and told him of my lost vision. Bob rushed over, took a look at my eye, then told Loretta to drive me to an eye specialist in Santa Fe. There I was examined by three eye specialists and by the end of the following week, I was scheduled for eye surgery. It turned out that I suffered a detached retina that required surgery immediately to re-attach it.

During the next year and a half, I had three surgeries on my right eye, and a fourth one for cataract removal on both the right and left eye.

In the end, my vision was restored, I got rid of my reading glasses and my vision is fine to this day.

The hidden blessing?

Well, you can draw your own opinion, if you want, but I would say the whole thing was an *eye-opening experience,* you might say.

I hadn't taken my diabetes seriously for about two years. I wasn't exercising or eating the right foods, and to make matters worse, I was drinking too much beer. When I lost my vision, I had the greatest wake-up call — for it told me, loud and clear, to change my way of life. Forthwith, I went on a diet, took up a daily walking regimen, though I have always been a walker, and determined that I was going to lose weight. The end result was that I lost 40 pounds and my blood count readings dropped way down.

Therefore, my conclusion is that, while the experience of vision loss was very scary, it, in a sense, needed to happen. To put it differently, this incident changed my life as much for the better as did my winning the lottery. In a manner of speaking, I won the lottery twice — first, the money lottery and second, the lottery of healthy living.

Ernie Thwaites, KFUN, and the War Censorship Department
(We credit Dr. Michael S. Sweeney.)
Some of the information for the following story comes from his research and writings, "Victory Unspoken"

On December 7, 1941, the Imperial Japanese Navy surprised the United States with a military strike against the naval base at Pearl Harbor. The following day, the United States declared war on Japan resulting in their entry into World War II.

This particular moment in our history is as well known as 911.

But perhaps what is not known is how the "day of infamy" as President Franklin D. Roosevelt termed it affected the everyday lives of many, if not all, Americans including myself. As the owner of KFUN, I have had an opportunity to see exactly how much our little town of Las Vegas was brought into the war.

Nineteen days after the Pearl Harbor attack, radio station KFUN went on the air with its first broadcast, Christmas Day. The station's owners and founders were Ernie and Dorothy Thwaites. Everyone I have talked to who knew Mr. Thwaites said he was a very intelligent yet demanding person. He was also known to be stubborn, opinionated and contrary in many ways. In short, no one pushed Ernie around. This, as it turned out, served him, and KFUN, very well.

With the start of World War II, the Office of Censorship ordered radio stations throughout the country to stop broadcasting war news in a foreign language.

Each week during 1943, the 250 watt transmitter of KFUN beamed ninety-two hours of news, music and entertainment into the thin, high desert air of Las Vegas, New Mexico. Listeners who tuned their dials to 1230 kilohertz heard the Office of War Information bulletins and the fifteen-minute Spanish version of Uncle Sam Speaks.

Ernie Thwaites didn't believe that KFUN needed to concern itself with the foreign language ban from the War Office. He believed that his transmitter, 275 miles from Mexico and three times that distance from the Pacific Ocean posed no threat to the nation's security.

Much of KFUN's audience spoke Spanish, a language that the Office of Censorship nonetheless classified as foreign. However, Ernie Thwaites believed his listeners' loyalty to the United States was beyond question. He knew that the ancestors of Las Vegas had colonized the area long before the Mayflower had landed at Plymouth Rock. The fact was, and is, that Spanish was not a foreign language to very many New Mexicans.

In March and April 1943, Edward H. Bronson of the Office of Censorship visited dozens of Southwestern radio stations to determine if they were complying with the voluntary censorship code. When Bronson returned to Washington, he told his superiors, Robert K. Richards and

J. Harold Ryan, that in his opinion the most efficient way to handle foreign-language broadcasts was to end them for the rest of the war.

Censorship director Bryon Price had at first decided before issuing the first edition of the voluntary code on January 15, 1942, that foreign-language radio stations "….furnished ready means of keeping various foreign-born Americans in touch with the country's war needs and aims."

Much later, President Harry S. Truman awarded Price the Medal for Merit on January 15, 1946, congratulating him for "distinctive and complete success" in his administration of censorship and simultaneous defense of freedom of the press. Price also won a special Pulitzer citation in 1944 for his work. After voluntary censorship expired on august 15, 1945, presidential press secretary Stephen T. Early told Price he should receive an award for "best performance of service to Government and Country in time of war."

But in his address to the National Association of Broadcasters meeting on April 17, 1943, shortly after Bronson's return to Washington, Price said he couldn't allow some stations to continue their defiance of the censorship and in his words, "One leak in the dyke was too many."

The battle between Thwaites and the Censorship Department continued for a long time. True to his nature, Thwaites stubbornly refused to comply. He also got his Spanish audience in an uproar about the issue and they flooded the Censorship Department with letters accusing the department of discriminating against Spanish people and their native language. Thwaites even wrote to the N. A. B., the radio industry's professional organization of which he was a member, asking that they support his defiance of censorship. That effort backfired and the letter found its way to Willard Egolf, a lawyer who was the N. A. B. 's public relations director, and he told the Office of Censorship about Thwaites' appeal on April 23 of 1941, Egolf felt there was nothing he could do but to advise Mr. Thwaites to conform and follow the war law. Thwaites' own attorney told Mr. Bronson that he too refused to represent KFUN in its battle against the censors.

By the summer of 1943, Mr. Price said the Office of Censorship was satisfied that foreign-language broadcasters had been brought into line. Bronson also found no code violations in monitored foreign-language broadcasters in four of the nine weeks between May 22 and July 17 of the same year. Accordingly, he told his superiors at the end of each error-free week he was hoisting the white flag of purity and virtue."

At this time, the only broadcaster who still wouldn't comply was Ernie Thwaites. He'd refused all requests for scripts and all monitoring of his Spanish programs. Consequently, Bronson, Ryan, and Price worked hard to coax Thwaites to change his mind, but they had no success. When contacted by the Censorship Department, Dennis Mitchell, the KFUN general manager at the time, describes Thwaites as notoriously strong-willed, as evidenced by his undertaking a successful, one-man crusade to have the local government pave a dirt road, (HWY 104) linking Las Vegas and Tucumcari.

Thwaites was proud of what he'd accomplished in Las Vegas. He'd built KFUN in 1941, lived in an apartment in the same building as the KFUN studio, and ran the station with wife Dorothy.

He was one man against the world when it came to the issue of censorship. On August 11, 1943, however, the office of Censorship decided it would wait no longer and told KFUN to observe the Code or discontinue Foreign Language Broadcasting.

Thwaites refused, accusing Price's agency of, "hampering, heckling and hamstringing" a small station. He said it would be impossible to prepare scripts and monitor his broadcasts, for to do so might bankrupt him, he said. In a defiant letter on August 19, Thwaites accused Price of trying to be judge-jury-and executioner and he ended with— "We know that our problem, in the light of world events, is insignificant.

Nevertheless, to us, whether we survive or not is 100% important! Moreover, there may be others who might feel as we do, that your threatened action is an unwarranted infringement upon Freedom of Speech and therefor a threat to our whole Democratic structure."

There could be some truth to this, since early on, Federal agencies began focusing on foreign-language broadcasters before the Office of Censorship was organized. James Lawrence Fly, chairman of the FCC, had sent FBI Director, j. Edgar Hoover a partial list of foreign-language announcers back in December 16, 1941, and Hoover shared the list with Mr. Price a week later.

Ernie Thwaites' letter was unique. Up to that time, no broadcaster had ever refused to do what the Office of Censorship had asked.

Price faced a dilemma. KFUN's unregulated broadcast might inspire a radio rebellion that would prove dangerous. If the code were relaxed on the claim that Spanish was a semi-official language, other stations might seek code exemptions for all kinds of reasons.

On August 24, Price dictated a memorandum that he believed would resolve the conflict. The memo included copies of the First War Powers Act and Executive Order #8985, which said, failure to comply to the Code of Wartime Practices could result in one of more of the following actions.

1. Imposition of mandatory censorship.
2. Enforcement of U. S. Censorship Regulations.
3. Recommendation to the Board of War Communications, established by President Roosevelt in September of 1940, to modify or suppress the activities of the station.
4. Recommendation to the FCC that the station license be suspended. Anyone convicted of evading or attempting to evade Section 303, faced a prison term as long as ten years, a fine as high as $10,000, or both. If the convicted person was the officer, director, or agent of any corporation, the law authorized the United States government to seize any property, funds, securities, paper, or other articles or documents, or any vessel, together with her tackle, apparel, and equipment, concerned in such violation.

Obviously, Price had him over a barrel, so to say. Reluctantly but wisely, Thwaites wired the Office of Censorship that".... Regardless of personal feelings, I will stop all Spanish programming on August 25."

Thwaites conceded only the battle, not the war. He informed his listeners that he was being forced to cancel Spanish broadcasting by federal bureaucrats in Washington. D. C.

However, Spanish programming resumed by February 1944, when KFUN's Spanish-language broadcasts were recorded and sent to the Office of Censorship. Those broadcasts led to another conflict, albeit a minor one. KFUN did not use the Office of War Information's Spanish news released about war bond sales. The Office of Censorship informed the Office of War Information of the omission, and it urged the station to air them. KFUN then sent a sarcastic note in reply. The Office of Censorship's records at the National Archives did not say whether the radio station eventually agreed to use the releases.

The Office of Censorship's careful handling of its feud with KFUN defused one of the potentially gravest crises in the history of voluntary censorship in World War II. If Thwaites had pressed his case, Mr. Price almost certainly would have compelled the station to comply with the censorship code or go off the air. If the dispute had gone to court, Price might have had to reveal, and use, his "club in the closet".......the attorney general's opinion that had given him the authority to control domestic radio through the legal definition of broadcasting as an international means of communication. Instead of legal restraint, however, Price had brought KFUN in line with public and peer pressure.

These two forces had changed the voice of radio during World War II, reducing the number of stations carrying any foreign-language programs from about 210 in the spring of 1942 (up from 200 on December 11) to 128 in the spring of 1943. Some had dropped German or Italian programs out of fear of offending their English speaking listeners. Others had stopped foreign-language broadcasts to avoid the costs of preparing scripts and paying program monitors. The Office of Censorship had brought about the change largely through peer pressure, patience, and pleading.

The long and short of this story is that sadly, Mr. Ernie N. Thwaites died in a plane crash in September of 1963 and his wife Dorothy died a few years later.

ACKNOWLEDGMENTS

Ernie and Dorothy Thwaites

I thank them for their foresight in establishing KFUN in Las Vegas. They could have chosen any other town in the state. Ernie was involved in the community and also was a candidate for New Mexico State Representative on the Republican ticket, running against long time State Representative David Montoya. Ernie was a licensed pilot whose life was cut short when his plane crashed in Edgewood, New Mexico just East of Albuquerque in September of 1963 at the young age of 59. Dorothy, his wife, died a few years later.

Founder of KFUN radio station. Mr.Ernie N. Thwaites.

Merle and Mida Tucker

The Tuckers bought KFUN and the property on KFUN hill from Dorothy Thwaites sometime in 1964 for a total of $135,000. The Tuckers were owners of KGAK radio station in Gallup. The Tuckers brought Dennis Mitchell to Las Vegas and hired him to manage KFUN. Merle Tucker was a Republican candidate for New Mexico Governor in 1946 when incumbent Democrat Jack Campbell sought a second two year term.

OPEN HOUSE at KFUN Sunday gave Las Vegans an opportunity to meet the new owners and personnel of the local radio station. Shown greeting guests are (l to r) Robert Adamson of Gallup, chief engineer of Tucker broadcasting stations; Merle Tucker and Mrs. Tucker, owners of Thunderbird Broadcasting Co. which recently purchased KFUN; Stewart Chamberlain, station manager; Lowell Christianson of Gallup, general manager of Thunderbird Broadcasting co. (Photo

Mr. & Mrs. Merle Tucker, (CENTER), owners of Thunderbird Broadcasting Co. were the second owners of KFUN/AM 1230. They bought the station on September 8, 1964 for a total of $135,000 from Mrs. Dorothy Thwaites. Mr. Tucker was a Republican candidate for New Mexico governor. The Tuckers hired Mr. Dennis D. Mitchell to manage KFUN. Mr. Mitchell was a former employee of the Tucker's.

Mr. & Mrs. Tucker. Second owners of KFUN and employees.

Carl and Patricia Mark

Carl and Patricia Mark bought KFUN and the land from Mr. and Mrs. Tucker in 1967. Carl Mark was a long time broadcaster, purchasing WTTM in Trenton, N. J. in 1948. He acquired KAKC/AM in Tulsa in 1962, and then obtained the rights to KACK/FM in 1963. Sometime in 1972 Mr. Mark established KLVF, the first FM station in Las Vegas. Mr. Mark retained Dennis Mitchell as manager of both KFUN and KLVF. Mr. Mark died July 4, 2000. His wife Patricia had passed away a few years earlier.

Mr. S. Carl Mark & wife Patricia were the third owners of KFUN. Mr. & Mrs. Mark then established KLVF 101/FM in 1972. Today it is Radio Station KLVF/FM 100.7 with 10,000 watts. Standing to the right is Mr. Dennis D. Mitchell.

Mr. & Mrs. Carl Mark third owners of KFUN/AM & founders of KLVF/ FM & Dennis Mitchell all dressed in western period clothes.

Dennis and Nancy Mitchell

The Mitchell's bought both KFUN and KLVF from Mr. and Mrs. Mark in 1991. Dennis Mitchell was first appointed manager of KFUN at the age of 34, by then station owner Merle H. Tucker, also president of Thunderbird Broadcasting Company and owner of two other stations. Mr. Mitchell was previously employed with radio station KRTC in Santa Fe in a commercial capacity and before that was program director of KGAK radio in Gallup, owned by Merle Tucker. Dennis is happy working at Wal-Mart in the electronics department and Nancy has retired as a school teacher with Las Vegas City Schools.

Mr. Dennis D. Mitchell & wife Mrs. Nancy Mitchell were the forth owners of KFUN & KLVF Radio Stations. The Mithcell's bought both KFUN/AM & KLVF/FM radio stations from Mr. & Mrs. Mark. Mr. Mitchell then sold the stations and the land to Mr. Will Sims & Mr. Don Davis owners of Meadows Media LLC. Pictured with the Mitchell's is film actor Henry Enriquez who visited KFUN.

Mr. & Mrs. Dennis Mitchell. Fourth owners of KFUN & KLVF.

Will Sims and Don Davis

Owners of Meadows Media, LLC. Business partners Will Sims and Don Davis bought KFUN/AM and KLVF/FM and the land from Dennis Mitchell on June 4, 2004. Will has owned and operated radio stations in Wyoming, Arizona and New Mexico, over a career of more than 40 years. He is past president of the Wyoming Broadcasters Association and was inducted into that association's Hall of Fame in 2007. He served on the National Broadcaster's Board of Directors and was once named a Jaycees International Senator. He grew up in Albuquerque, lived in Santa Fe, New Mexico for 25 years and now resides in Luquillo, Puerto Rico with his wife, the lovely Gabriela.

Mr. Will Sims, (left) and Don Davis. Fifth owners of
KFUN & KLVF. Owners of Meadow's Media.

Joseph P. Baca and Loretta A. Baca
Sixth owners of KFUN & KLVF.

We bought KFUN/AM from Meadows Media LLC in February of 2006, and then bought KLVF/FM in May of 2009, and also own over 24 acres of land on KFUN hill. In the first four years of ownership, we have invested over $300,000 dollars in new equipment and improvements in our stations. Our overall goal is to someday develop the land on KFUN hill to attract new businesses to the community and to build a new building for both stations on the Southwest corner of our land. We extend a spirit of gratitude to Ernie and Dorothy Thwaites for establishing KFUN in Las Vegas, and to all the former owners of KFUN and KLVF for preserving the stations. Without all of these people, Loretta and I would certainly have never had the opportunity of owning the stations. We are proud to say that combined, KFUN and KLVF have served our community and Northeastern New Mexico for close to 110 years. Thank you universe for such a blessing and privilege. We also thank Community 1st Bank for believing in our dream and for their financial support of our business venture.

J. P. Baca adding finishing touches to his book.

I believe I have had a love relationship with KFUN radio since I was a small child. During the beautiful New Mexico summer nights, my brother Fred and I would spread out a big mattress on the front porch of our home and sleep outside. In between giggles and bursts of joy, we squirmed as we told each other stories of the wicked crying woman, known to all youngsters as, *La Llorona*.

Though many versions exist, story goes, the old woman would roam alleys in the dark of night crying for her children whom she had killed. As she walked from one cemetery on the south side of town to the one on the north end, her loud haunting cry sent shivers throughout the neighborhoods.

Half a block west of our house was the old *caliche* where children played by day. But Fred and I knew beyond a shadow of a doubt, that this was where the old woman lived by night. At least, that's what our young impressionable minds believed. We were also sure *La Llorona* could come for us on any night she pleased as we slept out on our porch.

Each morning we watched as the vibrant orange and red colors of an early New Mexico sunrise embraced the horizon to the East. We marveled at God's early morning creation. The cool New Mexico air, singing birds, and barking dogs in the distance helped to wake us up. We then turned on a small radio we had placed on the cold concrete slab on our porch and listened to the Spanish program on KFUN, which started at 6: a. m. every morning.

We lay there, my eyes fixated on the mesa facing east where KFUN stood with its beaming tower looming over the sleepy town. We listened as the neighborhood came to life with Spanish music over KFUN blaring from radios in many adobe *casitas*. The smell of potatoes and bacon frying over a wood stove embraced the morning air, flavored by the sweet smell of fresh green chilé from Hatch, New Mexico, along with the smell of fresh tortillas and hot coffee. This was more than two hungry young boys could stand. In the kitchen, we found our dear mommy preparing the morning meal that would get us through the day. These are wonderful heart warming childhood memories of our mother that Fred and I and all siblings, hold dear to our hearts. Bless her heart and memory forever.

Here is a brief history of my home town.
The original, Las Vegas, New Mexico
(New Mexico Tourism Department)

Experience the spicy mix that New Mexico is,- - - from ancient Native cultures to the piquant blend of Hispanic and European traditions. The art, the soul and the stories that are New Mexico, reside in our museums, legendary historic sites, and majestic monuments to a time long past. We welcome visitors to the enchantment of our past, our present and our future.

The original Las Vegas, New Mexico, (Nuestra Señora de Los Dolores de Las Vegas Grandes). *Our Lady of Sorrows of the Meadows.*

Las Vegas is a rich and historic city with a vibrant past. In 1823, King Ferdinand VII of Spain wished to show his appreciation to his loyal subject, Luis Maria Cábeza de Vaca, (Anglicized to Baca), and made a royal land grant of 500,000 acres in New Mexico, (*Las Vegas land grant,*) to Don Baca for himself and his 17 sons and the 800 head of horses and mules that Baca owned. *Note* Luis Maria actually had a total of 26 children, (girls and boys), as a result of having married three times. His first two wives died as a result of illness. Don Luis Maria Cábeza de Vaca was eventually shot and killed in 1827 by Mexican soldiers in Peña Blanca, New Mexico where he and his family had a home. Eventually, a determined group of residents from San Miguel Del Vado, New Mexico, petitioned the government for the Baca land grant for the purpose of establishing the Town of Las Vegas, which was eventually established in 1835. In exchange, the Baca heirs received five other locations for giving up the land where Las Vegas sits today, and the rest is history.

Hermits Peak, at 10,263 feet overlooks the city below, which is nestled near the heart of a spectacular wilderness area, sweeping fresh lands, fascinating historic sites and wonderful national parks, lakes and rivers. Once the principal town on the Santa Fe Trail, Las Vegas reflects its rich history through its historic districts which boast over 900 historic buildings listed on the National Historic Registry, (more than any other city in the U. S.). The well preserved, late 1800s architectural styles are an array of Victorian, Greek revival, Queen Anne, Italianate, and Romanesque.

Visitors can stroll with ease with the past and the present.

Located off I-25, Las Vegas is only one hour Northeast of Santa Fe, 123 miles from Albuquerque, New Mexico and 327 miles from Denver, Colorado.

With a population slightly over 16,000, Las Vegas is known for its quality educational institutions of higher learning. New Mexico Highlands University, first established in 1893 as New Mexico Normal School, was then named New Mexico Normal University in 1902, and then became New Mexico Highlands University in 1941, as it expanded its role beyond teacher education. Las Vegas is also home to Luna Community College, and two secondary school districts. We are proud and fortunate to have as our neighbor, the Armand Hammer United World College of The American West right in our back yard. UWC is one of 10 such colleges located in countries across the globe. The only one in the United States, is located in Montezuma, New Mexico, just a short distance from Las Vegas.

For History buffs

Las Vegas is home to the Theodore Roosevelt Rough Rider Memorial Collection and Museum. Las Vegas is one of two cities in New Mexico to preserve its original Dale Carnegie Public Library, and today the building stands in its original state. We are the only city in the Land of Enchantment that still has an original Harvey House in the railroad district.

For out door recreation

Las Vegas offers year round golfing at the New Mexico Highlands University "Gene Torres" golf course. Fort Union National Monument, an important site on the Santa Fe Trail, first established in 1851. Visitors and locals enjoy the Montezuma Hot Springs year round. The Gallinas and Pecos National Monument and wilderness areas attract thousands of people for fishing, hunting, hiking, mountain biking, day and overnight camping and sight seeing. Our Nation Wildlife Refuge, located on NM Hwy 281 just a few miles east of Las Vegas is a big attraction year round.

The fertile valley of Las Vegas, known as "the Meadows," was occupied as early as 8,000 B. C. by Paleo-Indians. Sedentary Pueblo Indians were present in the area during the 1100s and 1200s until forced out either by drought or the pressure of Apache Indian attacks. Nomadic Plains Indians, and later, Comanches, camped in the Las Vegas area on their way to raid the village of Pecos and the other Pueblo and Spanish settlements to the west. A succession of Spanish explorers, such as, Alvar Nuñez Cabeza de Vaca, and Coronado who passed through Las Vegas in 1541, were on their way in search of the fabled cities of gold.

In 1821, the Santa Fe Trail came through the center of what became Las Vegas. When the town of Las Vegas was founded in 1835, the trail continued to occupy what is now Bridge Street, the historic Plaza park area and South Pacific Streets. These three routes are designated as part of the National Santa Fe Trail.

That is a brief look at the original Las Vegas, New Mexico.

I end my book with the following:
We cannot change the past, but rather embrace it, be thankful for the lessons life sends our way. Overcome, spread our wings and fly high, as you were meant to do.

In a humble spirit, I say, may my book be a blessing to all that read it, as it has been for me while writing it.

I willingly give up my past, and I am at peace.
(Author unknown)
Thank you Gerry and Loretta Hausman for your friendship, inspiration and editing of my book.
To all members of the Green River Writers workshop. I thank you for your encouragement.

Blessings. J. P. Baca

Made in the USA
Charleston, SC
18 August 2011